Forever and Always A Girl

by Hung Huynh

May 2022

Table of Contents

Editorial

Life is tough. Most of us have to think about money, career, and life in general. If you are born poor, it sucks. If you are lucky enough to be born into wealth, spending sumptuously also gets old after a while.

What is happiness anyways? Many have tried to define it for centuries. Sometimes, we look back at our lives, our choices, and try to find that equilibrium point where we can really find happiness to help guide us in life.

Born transgender, I learned so much about being true to myself. Yet, it was through so much pain, self-searching, fear, anxiety, ostracization, and much, much soul-searching and much courage to take a leap to become who I really am. When a kid, 4-5 years old, I would play with dolls instead of toy cars; I socialized more with the girls than with the boys in kindergarten. I lived in the 1990s where the society was not that liberal to recognize transgender children, let alone in Saigon, Vietnam where I was born, conservative Asian traditions still played a much more important role. Discrimination against trans children was deep; many doctors believed that being transgender was a temporary mental dysphoria, whereas the problem is in the body, and not the mind. Transgender was not recognized; transgender children and individuals were always "unofficial" and open to discussion, mockery, the black sheep among the herd, a shame for parents and a subject of fun so people could feel better about themselves. You had to hide.

My K-12 years, naturally, were never really happy. Kids would often bully each other at school for everything, and being transgender was no exception. In a competitive environment, such as where I was throughout middle school and high school, it was also a hurtful slur that many used to bring me down because I was better than them, albeit just academically. My frail body was no match for the boys; my figure did not have that bosom look of a normal female teenager in the blossoming years of her life; nor was I allowed, or had the courage, to express myself as a female, a young adolescent girl and budding young woman that I felt effervescing in my soul and my body; this sensation of my femininity in the regard, the look, the gestures, that I only wanted to leave them to develop naturally, instead of curbing them, correcting them in order to pretend that I was a boy when I was sad, and mortified even, to be placed among the boys when the group of girls was standing separately. I belonged to the girls, to be with the girls, and I was happy that way than staying with the boys, much as I admired them for their masculinity, their boyishness, their funny gallantry of the growing boys and lofty expectations they were learning to acquire as they became men.

Yet, my life did not turn into a sob story because of that. Perhaps it would, if I just accepted it, if I just buried my soul deep inside and pretended to live a lie for the rest of my life. Yes, it would have turned out like that if I lied to myself, to everyone around me about my gender, about who I was, about the girl blossoming inside me and showing me how to be a feminine woman with all the tricks, the coquetries, the highness, the meanness, the pretentiousness, and the kindness of being a woman. Far from it. From the insider perspective, I thought I turned out pretty well the moment I realized that, "This is my life". No one else was going to live it for me, and I had the power to make choices and seek opportunities to shape it for the better. It was simply a medical condition not well-understood by the society for me. They imposed their own norms and values, for what they did not understand or thought they understood already, but what they believed was wrong and I was the exception that challenged their conventional science; I was the exception that showed how imperfect their science was. Rather than finding a way to perfect it, they decided to put me aside to make their science universal, impeccable, unmistakable, and "exact". It was tough for sure; I could not blame them. Maybe I could, but I did not, because I was a child, a chicken; I was afraid. I was afraid that my voice was so small that nobody could hear me. I was afraid that even if they heard me, they would put me aside, ostracize me, ridicule me, make fun of me. They could not see it this way: that being born transgender was simply a medical condition, a physical imperfection that could be treated so the individual could be who they are and live normally, i.e. live their own lives without this gender anomaly bothering them or anyone.

I am a woman, born with this corporal imperfection, but the important thing that changed my life was when I realized that.

We are all born with different circumstances. Who says that being born poor is the end of it all, that poverty will perpetuate no matter how hard you try? Who says that being born rich means that you have it all, that the sadness and the boredom of existence will never hit you, and that you will stay wealthy your entire life? People do not say their problems, but that does not mean they do not exist. The important thing is, as people have always repeated, *"find your own peace and happiness"*, personal happiness from the inside. But happiness is an abstract concept, and how do you get it anyways?

If you are looking for a soap opera about a transgender woman talking about how hard it is to be born transgender, and expect me to write at lengths about it, this book is definitely not for you.

If you are however looking to read to understand it better, and how, despite being born transgender, I have come to live my life as who I am by seeking ways to change my circumstances, what I have found about the meaning of being true to yourself, what it means to be a woman, and how you too could benefit from learning about my experience to live your own life, a happier, more meaningful life, regardless of the woes you were born with, then read on.

About Me

My name is Hung.

I obtained a B.A in Economics and French from Ohio Wesleyan University and an M.A in International and Comparative Education from Teachers College of Columbia University. I also spent my junior year in college with Sweet Briar College Junior Year in France.

Chapter 1
A girl at heart

*

*   *

As early as three or four, when I could recognize more the world around me other than my parents, I realized I was different. I was naturally attracted to activities for girls. I liked pretty things, decorating and interior design for my dollhouse, braiding my blond-haired dolls and cradling them to sleep. I also had many plush teddy bears and a tiny plastic one that I loved to bite his tiny crunchy nose. They were my close friends. I also loved organizing social events for my dolls.

Psychologists theorize how gender is formed; I lived it. I had no interest in the tanks and helicopters and the hero toys my parents bought me. I was who I was. Yet, that was how they assigned my gender, because of how my physique was.

I never noticed any differences in treatment. I guess I was born in a good family, with kind, caring, loving parents. Certainly, I grew up to disagree with them, a lot, but I was doted. My parents cared for me and purchased me not only boys' toys, but later, I found, also dolls and Barbies, because they were what I was attracted to and naturally was inclined to playing. I found out, later on, that some of my aunts and relatives, were critical of my parents because they thought my parents were too permissive and doting, and purchasing these girly toys would make me "gay". I guess I have to thank my parents now, for letting me be happy and accepting me as a child and did not take them away from me.

Yet, what happened at home was comforting; going to school was a rude wakening of the reality. When I started school, socialization was not always fun, if not belittling. I did not know how they got the cues, but I was often picked on for being who I was. It could be because of my frail body. It could be the feminine way I spoke, talked, and explained myself. It could be because I played with the girls in girls' plays and was totally detached from the boys and their fighting, warfare roleplaying and futile running. Perhaps I challenged their normal perception of boys and girls, but I grew distant from others because of the alienation and the hurtful, and simply false remarks, that I was a boy who only played with girls. I did not care that I only played with girls. I cared that they called me "a boy," when conceptually, I was not that in my mind. I hated my body, but did not know how to explain my situation to others, or had the courage to tell to them that I was actually a girl. I had no real "proof" other than my behaviors and natural tendency, and explaining such a thing to people who would not understand it was not easy for someone of my age.

I was very fortunate to go to some good public schools, the children were well-educated, and would not do anything violent toward me other than the teasing and occasional moral harassment. Some were actually polite towards me, though it was an acquiescing kind of courtesy. Sometimes it was so hard for me to pretend, because everyone considered me as a girl anyways, so I just relaxed and be myself, to further accentuate the already well-formed judgment about me. It only hurt when they said that I was a "boy" or called me names for being a "boy who plays with girls" that the rude wakening of my situation suddenly dawned on me and saddened me for something I was too afraid to say, that I was a girl. In elementary school, I had a friend. He was boyish and more mature than the other boys at school. When I was about 8-10, he confessed to me that he liked me, and reproached me for making him "gay" and attracted to me. I remember those innocent eyes. I was bemused, and yet, happy. In my mind though, it was perfectly normal: A boy who says he likes a girl, what is the problem? I was more demure than the average girl at school, dressed decently and showed good manners toward others. I also considered myself the top of the pack, with superior sense of self and morals and values. As a girl, it was perfectly natural for me to receive that kind of attention. I was also a proud and mature person, more precocious than most children of my age after all. Yet, I could not let it be felt exactly because of my very situation. At the same time, I was glad because at least there was a boy who liked me instead of bashing me or making fun of me for something I had no control over. I guess I was fortunate in that sense having those people as friends and let me live the coquettish girl's life when all around me saw me differently.

*

*   *

I did not really like Saigon, where I spent my childhood, but I guess I was more because of the conservative culture there and it made being transgender even more difficult. There was no medium, no role model, no medical centers, no adults, no doctors, no nothing to show you a way out to resolve it. It lived buried in you, and as a child, I did not have the capacity to see that there was actually a way for you to change yourself physically, to be treated medically, and to live yourself correctly as a girl. The country had a bad reputation as a socialist country, ravaged, poor, even though in the city, you did not feel it that way. I thought I lived a pretty normal life with all the amenities you could find in a modern society. It was like a small American city, with all the buildings and services and access, but the reputation accorded to the whole country. I guess Saigon was once a very flourishing city, a hubbub of the West and Asia, so it was not that bad.

Strangely, it was what made me somewhat disconnected with the city. My parents were loving and tried hard to give us a comfortable life. I was fortunate in that regard. Beyond the household door though, it was a different world. Rules and expectations were the norms in the Asian popular culture mindset that I could never get used to. The Vietnamese were a group of smart people, but they were conceited, far behind the world in many ways, but they were proud because they just succeeded in gaining their independence. Now only comes public administration, and that was the difficult part when the ideological battles of the Russian-French socialists, criticized in the West, were what they concurred with and chose to experiment in the country for their freshly gained independence.

Saigon, however, had its own charming, old, quaint little qualities in my memories. The wheels rolled fast on the narrow street; the high old lean oil trees, the *Dipterocarpus alatus*, native to the region, with their pinwheel brown dry flowers falling down from the tall trees in the Fall. Saigon River elegantly shifted her gigantic body, moving to the Pacific Ocean and shimmering in the sunlight, along the docks where my Dad would often drove me around for a promenade on a late afternoon. Vibrant, with thick lines of motorbikes, it was a young city, growing with all its strength, energy, pace, and its own faults. The beautiful boulevard ran straight along the docks of Saigon Harbor.

Vietnam's social structure seems to be cut in half. Hanoi, the North, embraces an elegant air of old French colony and a somewhat conservative streak of pure Socialism, which subjected the region even more to the older thoughts. Saigon, renamed Ho Chi Minh after 1975 in memory of their revolution leader, in contrast, resisted from the socialist ideas and was more receptive to the old capitalist ideas fervent in the city since the Americans came to establish a democratic Vietnamese government in the South. The city built itself on high towers springing up into the sky and a myriad of newly-built structures amidst old buildings. Everything seemed shifting forward, dragging itself through the passage of time, the resistance of the new and the nostalgia of the glorious past. Everywhere seemed crowded. In fact, one of the most thought-provoking puzzled the City Council had to deal with was over-population, whereas approximately eight millions people lived on the surface of a 2600 kilometer squares area. Yet, the influx of people, mostly Vietnamese from poorer, less prosperous, rural areas, provided a labor rich enough to satiate the growth and the fast technological absorption of the city. Along the docks, large cargo ships arrived and departed. Sirens whistled out for coal, foods, goods, textiles, raw materials, and oil. Importation and exportation. Twenty years ago or so, Saigon was administered by strict regulations of the socialist government. The population was poor and not well-trained, disparaged by the war and discontent with the new government that interrupted their prosperous, peaceful life in the South, not to mention the exodus of South Vietnamese who fled the country in fear of the new regime. Saigon was like an old, shielded kingdom, living on its past of a democratic Vietnam. Failed policies from the new single-party government only accentuated the fear. With living standard degradation, even worse than before the Vietnam War, famine and poor management, in 1986, the country decided to change, for the better. All probably began from there to see the Vietnam now. Yet, after war ravage and 10 years of failed public policy, Vietnam found itself left far back behind other countries in the world. Saigon, once an envy of South-East Asia, was nothing to compare with leaders in the region. Yet, the city found its past an inspiration to work and restore the glory it once had. In contrast to the old methods, modern equipment and new, better technology was freely accepted into the city. Foreign companies were allowed to be in. So were foreigners, foreigners with skills and abilities to transform the country. After years of changing and improving the trading- laws and restrictions, the city now shrugged its old skin and appears in a newer, modern look. The city now can be seen with tall buildings in replacement of the sub-standard apartments left unfurnished for some fifty years, long roads substituting old red-earth passages, and trying to improve its management in line with the rest of the world.

Modernity coalesces with the ancient elegance of conservative Asia in this city. Along the piers, many restaurants and hotels, built long before 1945, still exist and preserve their original beauty. Neoclassical architecture imprints on many buildings. Traditional values still play a crucial role, reminding one of the old past. Every day, when school ends, students burst out in blocks, talking, laughing, discussing, and enlivening the roads even more with innocent youth. They try to keep the self-esteem and tradition alive, for good and for bad.

"Move on! Move on!" After all, the past is the pasts, and one has to move on.

*

*   *

For some reason, the Vietnamese culture was very challenging for me. I could never fit in, perhaps because of the reason I told previously, that I was afraid of a conservative country like Vietnam, burdened by a bad reputation government and a dearth of knowledge or information anywhere here about transgender individuals and supporting resources. People thought I wanted to see the world. Yes, it was nice. But I guess I was mostly because I could not live longer in a wrong body and pretend to stay outside of all the boy-girl matters at school. The worst of all was having to act as a boy, and somehow it was just sad. I wanted to shout it out to them all at the time to tell them who I was, but I could not. I was afraid of the Vietnamese society with their conservative values and lack of everything I could know to find myself and be a girl. I was afraid of living forever in a boy's body and suffocated in it. The only trans-women I heard of were those who fled to Thailand, had a botched operation, looked terrible, and came back to work as prostitutes and "street artists" in the pity, scorn and uncertainty of such choices, and a lack of protection from the government when all the paperwork just said they were "male" even after their operations. It was a stifling society, a stifling choice, a stifling place where they somehow survived on collectivism, traditions and values when they probably did not really know what they meant.

At 16, I wanted to be among the best young women, to gain admiration from guys, and to be an exemplary feminine figure at school, as many young women would dream of doing, but my situation played against me and forced me to be quiet. I had to leave.

I had to create the life that I wanted because no one would do it for me. High school graduation was an opportunity. I brooded the idea to escape from this country. I would be legally responsible for my own life. I hated living in my bodily prison for so long. They say time flies fast when you are happy, and it goes for eternity when you are suffering. Imagine that I did that for 18 years. No perhaps just 15, because I was not conscious of the brutal social pressure when I lived at home, a child. But those 15 years were nothing fun, when, captured in the Asian culture, it was just pitiful. I really had no friend to trust with this kind of matter. Back in kindergarten, it was easy. I just played with my female friends; we looked at the boys playing warriors going to imaginary wars, and had our own other occupations. But the more I grew up, the more I had to distance myself from all that. I could not perform as a boy, but I could not fully reveal myself as a girl either, so I had to play neutral. My body said one thing and my mind told me something else. I was a genie in the bottle, waiting to be released (Yes, that Christina Aguilera's song). I had no place to hide but the solitude of myself. I buried myself in schoolwork because that was the only thing that really gave me an escape from thinking about this, and the only solution out in my life. I made some friends, talked to people, but when the age of first love blossomed and boy-girl matters were hot in the conversations among adolescents of my age, I rescinded; I pretended to be this innocent, well-preserved, well-educated, and well-shielded from all the mundane banalities and strangeness of adolescent concerns. I was a prude, but only to hide from all that happened between boys and girls and the natural development of human beings. The funny thing about socialization was that being excluded was not as bad as being ridiculed for not participating. They probably thought I just did not care or was just pretending to be cold and anti-social. Of course I wanted to have a normal life as a girl that I was. I just could not, because I had to carefully craft my mind and my appearance, to stay away from any socialization lest I betrayed myself. I wanted to be free. I wanted to be a normal young girl as who I really was, that's all.

Sure, being transgender was tough and uncomfortable. Yet, what would complaining do? People would say, "I am sorry", "How does it go?", "It must be hard", "I don't understand it- Explain it to me". They applaud you for your courage or politely criticize you for your decision, even when they are not you and cannot really understand you. But will that do anything? Will they help? Will they offer any intelligent solution to resolve this problem? And what can they do in a situation like this anyways? People have remained transgender for years till the day they die. I was terrified of that prospect, having to live like that till the rest of my life, for simply being born in a certain way. Fortunately, I did not have to, and I am forever grateful.

In the end though, it is still *you* who will have to stand up and fight on your own on certain battles, because they are *your* battles. Overcoming my own fears, the uncertainty of life, of the lack of knowledge and information, when everyone around me did not know about this and was just as ignorant and confused as I was, or even more so, about this subject, was the biggest thing that helped me forward to find my way.

Upon reflection, I think it could have been positive. It made me more understanding, more sympathetic, more empathetic with people who suffered from some defects they were born with through no fault of their own. I guess I was lucky, because at least, there was a way out for me; I only did not realize it soon enough to act upon it sooner. But there was a way for me.

I was afraid of telling the world who I was. I was afraid to tell that I was a girl and that I deserved to wear dresses, to be attracted to guys and that I was perfectly normal as a girl. I hated dressing like a boy, even in the most neutral outfits of them. Yet, I was also afraid of being rejected, but more so because saying such things exposed me to violence and physical attacks. I was afraid of being asked out to leave the home by my parents, or being told to go through some conversion therapy for who I really was. No one could understand that but me. No one could solve that but me. Me and the doctors, obviously, but the doctors would not do anything or be able to do anything if I do not come forward to say what the problem was.

Fortunately, I figured out that I would rather stand up to be who I am than die in a lie, too afraid to be who I am and bury my own self till the day I die. I want to get out and fight for my freedom. Many transgender people lived till 40, 50, 60, or even 70 before making that decision to transition. Or never at all. It was not too late, but it could have been sooner. And what a sad pitiful life to live a lie like that. It was the scariest thing about being transgender that no one told you: being trapped forever in that wrong body, that wrong genitalia, that wrong self, and everything is wrong and will forever be wrong that way because there are no doctors, no one who can help you get out of that trap.

And that was why I came to America. For me, America was freedom. America was the Salvation place where I could be who I was, where I could find a solution to fix that internal physical, biological problem I was born with. America was accepting. America had the solution so I could naturally and quickly find myself again. Obviously, the reality was different. America was more difficult than I imagined, even more so than in the mind of an 18-year old teenager. But there was hope. There was hope that there might be someone who understands me and someone who can find a solution to fix that problem of mine. It was uncertain, but there was hope in that young mind of mine, and that was all that mattered.

Chapter 2
The Californian Dream

I had some relatives that I lived with in Oakland when I first arrived in the US. They were very kind people, and I loved San Francisco and the Bay Area: the sun, the beach, the ocean, the hills, the bus, the cable cars, poverty, the ghettos and the marijuana smell when you walked by their neighborhoods, but most of all, the freedom.

I went to a small community college there. It was strange at first, since I went to the very best public schools in Saigon, South Vietnam and also was among the top students at school. The school itself was historic, because Marguerite Duras's adaptation of her French colonial novella, "The Lover," was shot at that school. Maybe I do not care that much, or too proud of that South Vietnamese heritage, but at least I knew that Marguerite Duras and Chantal Goya, two of the most celebrated French people, were born and raised in Saigon. I was proud in that sense to be among them, although my identity, after years of living abroad, has effaced that birth identity- culturally speaking- and made it no more than a birth place in my social identity.

I applied to a bunch of American colleges during my senior year back when I was still in Saigon. Obviously, I did not know anything about colleges, and there was no guidance back then, and coupled with the insecurity of someone from a small fallen city, fallen to the hands of the Communists and figuring out each and every way to run away from that controlled society, I ended up applying to the top schools in America back then- Princeton, Vassar, Grinnell, and one last school I forgot—and was rejected by them all. In retrospection, I think I wrote a very conceited personal essay, when I did not mean to be conceited, in order to impress. It ended up being tossed in the trash, and people who read it must have thought how much of a pompous, insecure person I was. It was quite a lesson. I, learning from this lesson, tossed that trashy essay away in my upcoming applications elsewhere. I got accepted to Singapore Management

University, a then young but well-respected school in Singapore. It was a saving grace. Singapore was not America, however, and I, wanting to run away from the Asian society where I imagined must have been overly conservative for a trans person like me, decided to withdraw my candidacy. A friend in my class probably got that spot because they contacted me and asked me about the acceptance and my intention to enroll; to which I said no. She ended up getting the spot, and became successful there in her own rights. It was good to know that your spot could help someone because you did not take it.

I ended up attending a junior college in Oakland, California, where I had some relatives. My initial thoughts were only to use it as a gap year, where I could take advantage of the school opportunities in America to work and study, before reapplying to a normal 4-year college. I guess I could have gone to an independent school. Schools generally do not consider those who have undertaken classes at the college level on a full-time basis as first-years. Anyways, it was an eye-opening experience. When the airplane hit California and the view of the San Francisco Bay appeared, somehow my heart was lifted with this joy and happiness. I had never flown before. My first flight was to America, and seeing the sunlight, the Bay, everything about this land known as America was beautiful and a saving grace for me.

The first cultural shock was not immediate, but happened gradually as I discovered and readjusted to the life in California. Used to living in a homogenous society back in Saigon, I was shocked and scared to live in a place like Oakland. It was nice, but I never had to deal with such diversity in social classes, and was getting used to living in the real life in America. I never ran into any unwanted situation. My cousin, who had lived there all his life, obviously experienced more than me, but I guess it was the culture shock. I never tasted America or freedom before; I guess it was strange. I had to figure out what was good and bad to protect myself and live. I never learned driving; I walked everywhere. I did not have a car. I did not know how to drive. I never knew how to do that. I did not know anything. I was so passive and waiting to be fed, afraid of crossing the lines, afraid of making changes back in Saigon. I thought going to America meant I would be soon living the girl that I was, that I would find a solution soon, perhaps a hospital that could treat me. Changes do not often come easily at those big places. Sometimes, it happens gradually, beginning with some people, some individuals, an individual even.

My aunt was some South Vietnam immigrant after 1975. I found out a hard truth that I never knew before: that her life in America was rougher than she could have wanted. She did not want to say that, partly to save some grace, partly also to not worry my grandparents and her brothers and sisters back in Saigon. Yet, she took me on, and that was what I am grateful for today. My aunt is a kind person, a Catholic, and tried her best to be the best Catholic she could, though her ability to work and live in English was limited. What I liked best about her was that she had a sweet Southern Vietnamese voice. She was articulate, observing, and very sharp in her judgment; she was capable of seeing things and making some sound judgment. The time came crashing when she had to move to America and restarted her life all over with all the social disadvantages. It was tough, but those Southern Vietnamese were a group of courageous people shaped by the fallen times.

Being a shy person, afraid of ostracization, never living on the street or under the bridge before, the specter of it scared me. I could not overcome this fear inside me, the scrutiny from people I know every day knowing what I was doing, and the immediacy of finding that "solution" that we later knew as "transition," was as urgent as ever. My aunt was conservative. She did not have that American spirit yet; she loved American liberty, but her heart was that of a South Vietnamese woman—strict rules and correct culture was part of her upbringing. Things like mine were not easy for her. She attempted to correct me even, much to my ire, and I was too shy to be demonstrative. Plus, I was boarding at her house. I should have moved out, or perhaps paid the boarding, but did only housework in exchange. I felt I was too young, too little, and that made it hard. After almost a year, however, I grew accustomed to the life in America, could get used to people, the resources, and the potential opportunities I could do by leaving. I plotted to leave for good, beginning with the college application that I already waited for too long to build this new life of mine independently.

I could stay, complete 2 years of study at that community college and transfer to a 4-year college, but then it would be so far-fetched from the deepest desire inside me to transition and become a true girl that I was by living in California. My cousin was like my closest friend. He was a friendly and understanding person, although obviously, I did not even tell anything about my personal desire to transition to him. I discovered that the Southern Vietnamese pre-1975 also formed a strong network there, helping each other out in America. Perhaps they were open-minded people, as I gradually learned over the years, but my impression was that their culture was still very Southern Vietnamese traditional, all the more in America where they were afraid to lose their identity. Living there would only make it more difficult for me with all the visits and obligations. I guess I could have run away and ignored them if I did not like it, but I was socially conformed around them; making a radical change to cut ties with all the past seemed impossible. Leaving for a new State, somewhere far away, seemed more tangible. At least, the transition could be gradual. I had to leave.

Chapter 3
College & Ohio

I was obviously filled with that invincible determination for freedom. I was so oppressed mentally to not do what I wanted, not daring to study what I wanted, not having enough money to study what I wanted, not having the medium to combine all the chances I could to see for myself and let other people see that yes, my way works. I was not this simple nerd, the worst of all, a boy nerd with female personality and behavior that they all secretly thought I was. They were wrong. I could talk. I could overcome the pure natal setback of not being born in America and had to find my way out to freedom and full expression of myself that they did not think I could. I was a girl with this burning fervent desire inside me to live the life of a girl that I really was. Sure, what is the purpose of that freedom anyways? Maybe it means little to them to be a girl or a boy, but that is my life and it is not theirs to tell me what to do and how I should spend it. If they were that caring, they could have freed that crazy social environment that wrapped us up in their arbitrary values and arbitrarily told me what I was supposed to do to act like something I was not. I think this is the hard part about adulthood: the role of school is to foresee the possibilities that could help us make the best decisions to our lives, but we still have to think critically and choose wisely. At the college level, professors and professionals are aware of that, should be aware of that. Their role, as educated parents and professionals, is obviously to nurture well their students and help them avoid all the bad roads they might fall into, but are also not afraid to let them explore their roads by showing them what is good and bad.

It was a wild freedom, the freedoms I had so yearned for and waited : freedom from all past relationships, freedom from fear, freedom to start doing what I wanted, freedom to explore, freedom to learn what I wanted to learn, freedom to get an education that I found wanting in what I had had. I was so happy to finally go to college, a real college. It was beyond the American movies I watched, those chic, learned, cultured people, confident, outgoing, and proudly American. I could start learning and enjoy that education too. My first year, I was already determined to embrace the liberal arts education offered, without losing sight of the reality by double-majoring in Economics in addition to whatever I could do there. I had always wanted to study literature. In retrospect, I could have gone fully wild: to only study what I wanted: purely literature. I could be extremely practical, and perhaps do Business Management, or Accounting instead of Economics. I did not see it that way however. It was my shortcoming. I did not know what business management was, and my idea of Economics was that it enveloped the necessary business courses that I needed to work in the real world when I graduated. Economics was the most practical thing I could think of to keep myself on the ground, when in reality, it was not. Economics was still theoretical, and it did not fit me well enough. Plus, I had to grind with math courses to take alongside with the aim of attending a doctoral program afterwards, just in case. I thought they went pair in pair in other to find jobs later on after graduation, at least upon searching online and seeing the different job descriptions for economic analysts or business-related jobs at different companies. Upon reflection, I should have just studied something that I really liked. Many a broad education was good, and encouraged in a liberal arts education, but even in a liberal arts education, there was so much more than just Economics that I could think of to set one major. Business management, with the hands-on approach to everything in business, from financial analysis to accounting to human resources and management, was probably something that I could appreciate more in the Economics Department, while allowing me to explore and develop my competence elsewhere and see my opportunities grow.

For when I did French, it was what procured me the most success and opened me the most doors in life with countless possibilities for me to grow and build my life, despite all the initial fears of the vagueness of my future of studying French in college. Most people would say something like French would lead to a road of unemployment; my experience showed me otherwise. I had the most challenging, and most exciting opportunities because I majored in French, what I loved best in college. It showed me that if you are truly interested in French and can combine your intellectual pursuit with a clear career direction to earn your life, the roads will open slowly and widely for you. And I realized that being truly passionate about French did not just open me the doors to a doctoral program in French Studies nor should it be the only road open to me. In fact, I used more of what I did in French than what I studied in Economics, simply because I did not retain much in Economics than what I could practically use from French, from the practice of the language in daily life, the conversations coming from the language and literature that I studied, to other work and higher learning opportunities. My interest and pursuit in learning something that made me happy provided me with an initial point of contact to communicate all that to people I met. I also found the numerous opportunities coming by learning French further. I think it was the genuine interest in French that earned me many opportunities in life, and I could communicate that to other people, and that was important. That was why, even though I double majored in French and Economics, I should have done French and Latin, or French and English, because those combinations could have been much more powerful in my case since I was sincerely interested in languages and verbal communication, philosophy and culture. They were also purely academic, but a solid foundation in academics that would give me the confidence I could have in knowing something well, and could put in real practice and use what I could use best to earn a meaningful life.

French was the most fun and enlightening classes I studied in college. My first French teacher, a retired Emeritus French professor that we lovingly called Madame Courtney, was the best I had at that school. She was funny, lighted up the classes with all little details about French culture and Paris and croissants and the French living style that freshmen and women like me were keen to know. I particularly was happy to attend each class, two to three sessions per week, not only because I was the best, the most active, but also because each class was new and fun to meet our kind-hearted and jovial Madame Courtney with her interesting discussions on everything to make the lessons, basic grammar and conversations at the French 101 course less tedious. Obviously not everyone agreed with me. Madame Courtney's exams were often considered difficult by many students in the class. I normally did well in all of my exams, so maybe that was how I was spared from that sentiment. Perhaps learning a second language was difficult. Regardless, I thoroughly enjoyed the French classes, and most notably with my first French professor Madame Courtney who gave me the initiation to the French language and culture and the University Hall at Ohio Wesleyan, with classrooms in that emblematic towering wooden castle that made every day a new joy and memorable experience for me. I still remember that classroom, in the corner, overlooking the greeneries around the school, that crackling wooden floor, Madame Courtney, and the faces of my friends. On rainy days, it was even more magical, so warm, so cozy in that white neon fluorescence.

With that fortunate initial encouragement in French, I went on to take more advanced classes in French. I studied French rapturously, literally fervently; I hated that I did not understand what people said in French yet, and it motivated me to watch the audiovisual materials available in the library, borrowed books from interlibrary loans, studied high school textbook materials that I thought my American friends had the opportunity to study but I did not because I was not born in this country, and used each and every occasion to utilize all the resources, the classes, the club, speaking activities I could to work on my French. I discovered French music, French history, French living styles as recounted in American textbooks and available resources at my School. I locked myself in the audio room downstairs in the library, that small corner with a VHS and DVD player, and a TV, and just watched those videos. The most memorable was perhaps a documentary about Grenoble. That beautiful place, the beautiful French culture that those rainy days reminded me of and just how peaceful & pure life in France-Grenoble was for me.

I also loved English. The Sturges Hall housed the English department. I always liked that Department. In fact, I thought of double-majoring in English. That could have been a nice combination that could fully explore what I was truly interested in, and could go far from there. Instead, after much consideration, I decided to keep a practical hand and chose to double-major in Economics. I also liked my Philosophy class, for some reasons, was housed in the Science Building for that class I took. It was fun. We discussed Hobbes' Leviathan, and reveled in some intellectual deep thinking in that class. To enrich my academic skills, and especially in languages where I thought was a major advantage of me, I also took a year of Spanish during my second year. I did extremely well; I earned mostly over 90 and sometimes over 95 for most of my exams and quizzes, while the rest of the class trailed in the 80s, even for the best of them who had taken Spanish since high school. Yet, I guess I did not like it as much. Initially, I wanted to take Latin, but somehow perhaps the professor was talking about a book that was weak, so I decided to choose another language. I thought of Russian, which was not offered back then. I thought of German, which coincided with another class I had. So I took Spanish. Well, my Spanish professor was a lovely lady, Donna Donnelly was her name. She saw that I took French, and was also a fun teacher. I guess I learned well that class, but it was not really my thing.

I continued to study French and upgraded my French by working independently that way all my years in college, and ever since. I had a job at the school's library, because a friend was releasing a few hours of her work, and so I had it. My supervisor at the school's library, Mr. Bernard Derr that we familiarly called Bernard, was French, so it was a big plus for me to say bonjour, au revoir and discuss about France and French. I guess it was that that made Bernard a friend of mine at school and at the library. Bernard was always funny, a gentleman, and typically French with his gestures and way of thinking that amused us at the library. When he retired, it was like something was missing from the library, when it was just work, work, work, and the collegiate feel was also gone. He worked in the Special Archives upstairs, so I got to see him now and then, even worked there briefly now and then to help with archival work.

By the second year, I was already eligible to take advanced level classes. I tapped in 3rd-year French classes, which made me very proud because I could start reading French Literature, the real, unabridged version, and that could be a new challenge for me in upgrading my vocabulary and reading French. It was also necessary: I thought about my junior year and yes, I wanted to study abroad in France. It had always been my dream ever since my first year in college, that fancy semester in France. It was the epitome of a college education for me, for, like every other American college student, it was like going to a foreign country, a country where you actually want to be, study, and revel. I felt like everyone else with that same excitement and eagerness to explore a new country, and enviable one because all my life I had been shoved down to take what was not wanted and made the most out of it. Could it be for once that I could do something that I wanted to do and receive just that, and nothing else? It was especially important to me: I really loved French. Maybe I had a chip on my shoulder, but I always felt American; I saw no difference between me and my American friends and yet I could tell the difference between me and the international students. I felt an American at heart, in my ambitions, my petulant ambitions and thirst for freedom that had always burned inside me. I knew poverty; I knew poverty in America; experienced it; when I was in California, unlike these new students from abroad who got to go to private schools in their home countries and flew directly to their private college. I had a taste of America. I lived like an American. My advisor once looked at me, and told me he was wondering, what was the difference between an international student and an American? I knew the smell of the marijuana when walking blocks and blocks of streets on my way home, the fear of shooting, the dirtiness, the rawness, the frankness and normal struggles of an American.

There were obviously two major obstacles: first, most study-abroad programs in France I saw required advanced level of French. Second, the finances. I was not this silly person thinking that I would be able to attend these programs for free. I had to work to earn money to pay for them, or at least find ways to fund them, winning a scholarship for example. I also came to Ohio Wesleyan with a merit scholarship. I wanted to carry that renewable fund to my third year, not at Ohio Wesleyan, but with my college year in France. It would be the same. Sure, some people said it was only a tuition rebate. Yet, schools had to fund their administration and normal business operations, but the calculations would be imperfect if just because I decided to spend my junior year abroad, I had to lose all that third year funding. Plus, studying abroad in France costs less than in the US. I would only be asking for a fraction of my merit-based scholarship to be used for my study-abroad program. And nicely, I thought it was also a policy approved by Ohio Wesleyan. I was only pushing it further perhaps when I applied to full-year programs.

I had to fight vigorously to get there. Apart from my applications to study-abroad programs, I had to talk to everyone at school, from my professors, to my international study-abroad advisor, the academic dean, because I was unsure they would transfer the money for me. I need it to fund my study abroad. I was scared of this failure: it would suck to not have that opportunity. One semester was not enough. I planned it out to spend a whole year in France, because I thought it was good enough for me to be fully immersed in French culture. I already declared my French major. It was only natural that studying in France for one year would show this commitment.

I received a partial funding from my school also earned an outside scholarship from the study-abroad program to finance it. It all came as a surprise. I was attempting to ask if I could transfer all my scholarship to the study abroad program, and did not get any news from my school's administration, when I found out I got accepted to all my study abroad programs and the best of all, received that extra funding from Sweet Briar College, the best and most desired study-abroad programs on my portfolio. I thought of yielding, and simply would only do a semester abroad, just a simple semester abroad, that was enough for me. Yet, I had one year. Doing French was right, because the opportunities at Ohio Wesleyan at the time, although were not much for Modern Foreign Language majors like me, were enough that I could push forward and reach out to the larger world what I could bring back to that community and to my own academic development.

It was all a flutter flying to France- for the first time. Everything was new and exciting for me. I had never been to France before in my entire life, and Sweet Briar College. Sweet Briar College evokes something feminine, refined, and pretty, at least something that I was proud of identifying with: womanly, girly, like those pretty classy young women in the 50s and 60s in their flowered shirt dresses. We visited different well-known places in France when we first arrived in France. We had a small introductory week in Tours, a small town in the Loire Region of France just West to Normandy. Tours was a classical old French town, with its water fountain in front of the Hôtel de Ville and flowered beds sparkling in the sunshine. We studied at a school called Institut de Touraine, a lovely little place with a nice old castle overlooking a broad spacious garden with old tall trees. It was perfect. It was like being transported back to the 19th century in a private home garden, and you can imagine playing your peaceful days there. I imagined when it rained, just lightly, it would be so clean, so fresh, so perfect. My host family was a history teacher and a boy of about my age. Arthur was his name. It was living an old French life in an average French family. On a weekend, they also took me to a priest's house nearby, and they talked while I also got to play in the garden with a kid there. That environment was so familiar with me. Just an old, average, no fuss, family life in France that I had a piece of. I also went to Church on Sunday, a small local Church, praying there, and it was nice to see, and pray in a local church on Sundays.

We stayed in Tours for only 2 weeks, then left for Paris. It was most exciting when we first came to the 14th arrondissement. The school was in the 6th, so we passed through some nice open pedestrian quarters where they had their local hospitals and wide boulevards. I took many classes at the numerous partner universities when we arrived, even taking private music lessons at a local school there. I only began taking violin lessons my sophomore year, just to learn something I wished I had taken before, so technically, I was a novice. Other American students in the program and I, we all initially had some difficulty adjusting to the French learning environment, but we all tried to figure out our own way to study and explore the city to bother too much about all this. I was chagrined at times because of the colossal amount of vocabulary and new learning methods that the French students had to study. I had to double even triple the amount of work at times, but it was worth it. I found it most useful because their classes were much related to each other, and the French students self-studied a lot as French universities were considered not that helpful or that great either way. They were for me, but I totally understand why they felt that way with the big universities and lack of attention that we were used to in America. My schedule was jammed between classes and excursions with Sweet Briar, classes with the French students at my public universities- branches of the la Sorbonne that was well-known in the United States but obviously normal public universities in France- as well as embarking on my own independent trips in the city. They had this very practical Pass Navigo, which allowed you to travel freely in the subway and buses everywhere without having to pay an extra penny- at something like 350 euros per year. It was very practical for me. I did not know I would get to go back to France again, so seizing each and every opportunity to be as French as I could was the dream I wanted to realize. Paris smelled good when it was cold in the winter in the metro line 10 where I would ride to school and back home in the 15th arrondissement. The host family was not nice, and picky and calculating; they obviously considered me just as a side boarder to share meals with and renting me that tiny *chambre de bonne* on the 6th floor, where I had to hike up every day from their chic apartment on the 2nd floor. Obviously, I was not happy and left after a semester. I burned, accidentally, the linens while doing my ironing, and that was some memory. Anyways, it was nice to finally be in Paris. I listened to Françoise Hardy in that tiny chambre de bonne, studying, and just imagining the life of a normal college student in a huge, expensive city like Paris. It was a nice ambiance, even in that kind of want. The city was sad for some reason, perhaps nostalgic might be a better word, but fortunately, with my natural inclination to make friends with French students ever since the day I was still watching videos about schools in France back in the US, I found them genuine and loving. One professor in literature at the Sorbonne also noted me out from the class for my writing. That made me happy. I also liked her class a lot—pure, clean literature, from someone you expected from an Ecole Normale Supérieure in France- one of the better-known schools where many talented students are attracted. I knew that I would have to give back to all these schools that gave me money and scholarships for college and all the fancy study-abroad programs later on when I retire, but I figured it would be worth it because of the opportunities they gave me. It is a natural thing to give back for the wonderful things people have given you in your life. I learned so much and had so much a memorable experience with them.

Day in, day out, it was like a dream. I savored each and every day in Paris with Sweet Briar College. It was a dream come true for me.

I met someone that was the hallmark of real love for me when I first came to France. It was instantaneous. That moment he appeared, the whole world seemed to just disappear. Stood before me was him and him only. It was like that face you had been longing to see all your life, pre-life and pro-life perhaps, suddenly appeared before you, the face that corresponded exactly to every detail of the one you should meet in your entire life. Search no more. The heartbeat, the environment, everything.

I made up excuses to see him. I remained contact. I invited him out to concerts, knowing that he also liked them. Seeing his face those days was the most beautiful thing that completed the picture of studying abroad in Paris for me. We only saw each other a few times, but it was somehow enough, more than enough to know him, and to see how wonderful it was to be with him.

I think he knew that I liked him. He just did not say it overtly. There were barriers between us. He was a regular, straight guy. I was a girl who could not say it. I was blocked physically, when mentally, I knew that I could say anything I wanted when I wanted to. It was all the back and forth like that that made it lingering, hard, and possible to move anywhere. It made me more determined than ever, however, to be who I was: just a real normal woman that I was meant to be born with. It was like they could see through me inside my soul for the woman that I was, but we were all blocked outside by this physical appearance that we all had to pretend to respect. No more. I was sick of it. I could not stand another day living a lie. I took the courage to tell my parents who I was. They were shocked. They disbelieved me. They came to visit me, asked me questions, but eventually nothing happened. They thought it was a phase, just something I said. I showed them around the city, and they really had that idea by going back to call me the name they used to give me, not respecting the new gender pronoun. I understood the strangeness, and tolerated, but it was a clear sense that I had to help myself. My parents could not help me. I had to help myself— it was that firm and positive. At least I dared to confront, the kind of necessary confrontation that sooner or later I had to respond. I wanted once and for all let it be known, so that my parents had no doubt and no shock about what happened. If they wanted to disown me, fine, but that was who I was. I could not live a lie. I could not be who I was not.

The response was positive. Maybe my parents were weak, or it was that they could not do anything about it and wanted to know. It was nice and relieving to let them know. They came to visit, and in exchange for that candidness, I had a relief in my mind to have an open and honest conversation with my parents about the issue. It was the first step.

I came back to the US to complete my studies after my junior year, and he seemed to pick up the signals and waited for me all those times. Maybe it was then that I realized, gradually, that he liked me too. I also told him. Yes, I told him I was born transgender. He did not say anything at first, but then he accepted to visit me over a dinner before I left.

I returned to the US after my junior year, and took time to really begin the procedure that was so little known to me. It was lingering to leave Paris, but I got out of the French spell once I came back to the US, meeting old, familiar people and getting back to everything that was big and generous in old, beautiful, frank, honest, and competitive America.

Once college was done, I also figured out all the necessary information to start carrying out my gender reassignment treatment. I carved out my plan, one by one. I could not wait anymore. People did not know, or had to know everything about me. I was in charge of myself, my own feelings, and perhaps, because I already told him, perhaps that was the only thing that mattered. He knew the truth about me, and for me, that sufficed; Certainly, God also knew. I did my confessions and prayers to God, so God knew, but outside of God, outside that sacred place, not many single mortals knew that hard fact about me. They could guess, but could they guess that I was in fact a girl and I refused to identify as anything else? Especially in a woke society, they wanted to say everything about me that fitted in their narratives. It did not matter. I was a girl and I simply just wanted to prove that. Everything was brewing during all that time in college already; now with more maturity and certainty, I slowly carried out the plan. I first met with the psychologists at my school to obtain legal documentation certifying that I was indeed a transgender, then found doctors to put me on the hormone replacement therapy. It would then enable me to find the surgeons for the confirming surgery. Paperwork was also necessary. It would be useless to not have this part figured out, and was part of the reason why I was discouraged at the beginning and delayed this project. Fortunately, at the time, laws and regulations became more inclusive of transgender individuals, and civil rectification was a possibility in the United States. I was still held back by the Vietnamese paperwork, because for them, I was still a Vietnamese national, and that dreaded me most years and years afterwards just knowing how this slow, communist regime put a toll on me with their backwards bureaucracy and manmade laws--- and not very smart men they were. I did everything I could however to stay away from them— a government I did not recognize as my own, a country where I had no cultural attachment other than a piece of paper which was more a burden than a blessing for me and my dreadful situation. Regardless, one could not expect everything to be perfect—or perfectly given. One could, however, work things out as one wanted. I worked swiftly at the necessary legal procedures for a legal civil change on my documents according to US laws. Money was also an issue, and a weighty one anyhow. Basic primary surgery for vaginoplasty ran between 50.000- 75.000 dollars in the US. I did not want to go anywhere else, for fear of leaving the US, I would have to use that dreadful, awful passport where my identity was wrongful given and yet they refused to fix it for me. For this kind of surgery, I did not want to see anyone simply out of discretion. I wanted to show myself anew, treated, as the girl that I was meant to be. I figured out the list of the doctors I wanted to see, saw their reviews, before narrowing down my options.

I gathered my courage to walk calmly to the health center at my school. The psychologist was a tall, swift, middle-aged man and had a calm demeanor. His office was small, comfortable, well-lit, and decorated with psychology books and magazines. He sat me down in a chair in front of him. We talked. I found out no one had ever come to talk about this before, even though they had held many awareness discussions on campus. I guess I was the first one. It was a natural, easy conversation. I already expected all sorts of reactions from people, and I also gathered enough confidence to tell him about myself in confidentiality and handle any spiraling situations, it really helped. I guess I was lucky. The psychologist calmly listened, and after a few conversations, adroitly followed all the necessary protocols to make the psychological assessment for me, enunciating and repeating questions every now and then to make sure that I was indeed transgender. After a few sessions, I obtained the paperwork I wanted.

I soon got the recommendation letter from him before the end of the fall semester when I quickly graduated from college to save some money and could effectively earn money, see the doctors, and carry out the plan that I was burning with desire to complete. I made several copies of that precious letter, saying how he, the psychologist, recognized that I was a sane and sound minded person and that I had suffered from what they termed, gender dysphoria, and that I could receive hormone replacement therapy and gender confirming surgery as treatment. I readied to find a doctor for my hormone replacement therapy. I moved to New York, then San Francisco. I should have stayed in New York, because I almost got a job there, but money running out, I ran back to California to stay with my aunt's family for a few months. This was when I had the courage, and the ability to look for medical resources to help me. I made a few timid visits to Lyon Martin Center in San Francisco, and at this time, began my hormone treatment. It was smooth. They did not ask many questions. They accepted what I said, and were very supportive in getting me on hormone replacement.

A few months after that, I flew back again to New York, this time for good after a short summer in Vermont at the French School of Middlebury College where I was accepted to their graduate program.

Chapter 4
The New York Girl

I guess my professors wrote me killer recommendation letters that
helped me pull it through. I got in UPenn, Teachers College at
Columbia, and King's College London. I was rejected by Harvard
and dropped NYU after receiving the early acceptance letter from
UPenn. Somehow Columbia University sounded like another dream
come true for me, just because I did French, even though in reality, it
must have been more than that. I felt an independent spirit; I was
intensely competitive, ambitious, but young and childish in
retrospect. Columbia was nice, because I only heard of it by name
and never had a chance to attend it. It felt right and nice to study at
an esteemed institution, although the reality, as I found out, was
much more normal than my own imagination. I had seen photos of
the Columbia campus before: the relaxed campus, Corinthian
columns and Roman inspired building structures in red bricks and
white marble stones with graveled Latin names on the front porch of
their library, was just a dream and a vision of liberty and
independence that for me was a big deal. It had a reputation of a
disparate school spirit and utmost individualism that many people
detested. It sounded so good to me. I was not exactly the kind of
sociable atom in the universe. The pride, the excellence, was in the
people, the individuals making up an ensemble, in the high quality
resources I could utilize at school for my academics. I was proud,
just an egoistic pride of associating with a reputed institution that
saved me much from advertising and marketing myself--- which I
later found out was only the initial door- the real work after that was
the same, of not harder with the judgment and expectation people
had for someone graduating from a school like Columbia, and the
sneer they had if you failed to live up to that expectation---I was a

person beyond Columbia. The fact that the school was just a small part in the integral magnificent landscape of New York City, was exactly what I wanted. I wanted to be free. I wanted to run into that city, mingle perfectly in the grandiose nature and constructions and the fabrics of that celebrated city where I never even dreamed of, or thought of moving to.

I had a large choice of graduate schools. I could also have gone to UPenn or King's College London, where I was also accepted, but it would not make any difference, because I wanted to be at Columbia. I wanted to be at this school, and explore New York City and learn about everything I could about this city, something that Boston, Philadelphia, or London would not offer me. London would be great, but it is not New York. People love Boston, but they are not me to know what I want. Boston seemed beautiful and romantic. It is the home of the revered Harvard after all. I imagined it must be so beautiful: men in white fedora hats and buttoned jackets strolling along the docks upon intellectual conversations; on a beautiful, sunny, dozy afternoon, students languishing on the pastures along the Charles River, where young college men rowed along the soft-set sweltry Bostonian sun. It was so beautiful, so much of a college town.

Fortunately, I wanted to live in real life. The allure of college already faded in me. I went to a very small school in a small town in Ohio. I loved it there, made some great friends and knew some excellent professors, and I loved the campus golden in crested fallen leaves in the fall. I had an excellent education; it was natural then for me to follow this experience with something big, something crowded, something amazing, careless, competitive, crazy, fearsome, and yet worthwhile. I wanted something like New York. I was glad I got in Columbia exactly because it was in New York; In New York, where the assumed culture was that one was free to do what one wanted; I could start being who I truly was without anyone passing judgment on me. Certainly, people were people. New York, a metropolitan diverse multicultural place, meant you had to find the right place to mix in. New Yorkers were just a mix of chaos, but in that chaos, you could find your own place to live. And that for me, was to be who I was, on my own. The church, the parks, the buildings, and sociological fabrics in this city... were all that I could use. I could just not care about anyone, vicious minds that only wanted to stop me from being who I was. No more of that. The first few days in New York, I walked around that neighborhood. I had been in New York in January, finding an apartment uptown, but I never really got to know New York or ventured downtown, or felt like a part of that city for lack of cultural anchorage. I was then. I strode along the Riverside Park. Yes, it was New York, its ambiance of green trees, sad rainy days stretching for blocks and blocks and blocks. It was New York. New York of the clichéd Times Square, but I also discovered Hell's Kitchen, Chelsea, Washington Square Park, and other hippy or refined neighborhoods. It was nice to learn to be part of the New York's cultural fabrics then.

The Columbia's Graduate School of Education, called Teachers College, had a strong reputation in education policy in the US. I found out however that sadly, it was used as a cash cow for the university. It was a bit very disappointing. Yes, my goal was not to only sit glued at school to learn. I wanted to explore the city, and school was only a part of it. The low quality of instruction and administration at this school was however off-putting. Being an affiliated institution with Columbia although it served as its graduate school of education, their "complicated relationship" with the university created a whole bunch of administrative problems, from the student ID card, email address, to cross registration and social identification with the Columbia community built inherently by the administrative model. Yet, fortunately, after spending a whole semester figuring out the ins and outs finding out about all the best professors and brooding a bit over the reality, I found out at least a safe corner in quality classes really gave the school the prestige and quality you would expect from an esteemed institution, those that are truly qualified professors that go beyond their personal Ivy League graduates. Taking classes with some of them was a saving grace for me. Dr. Heubert at the time for example, was someone I learned well from. I at least could combine my interest in law and policy to work on subjects that were useful and intellectually stimulating.

I learned that other Columbia Schools, SIPA, Engineering, Arts and Sciences, Law... were not essentially better. I could have applied to SPIA, their school of international affairs. It was probably a good choice however, because the tuition was higher there and the rate of international students and professors was also extra-phenomenal at that school. Some were highly qualified, but some said it was purely an image because classes were large, instruction quality was low, and it was very costly. They had to pay to do some internships. I found the idea of paying to do an internship ridiculous, so never bought into that idea. They do not have to deal with the same administrative problems as Teachers College, but they also had the same problems in terms of quality. I also stayed at a graduate dorm called International House nearby, which charged you money for meals and you were forced to pay for them, but at least they offered some rebates so the rent was more or less affordable, compared to independent renting where it was hard to find if you were new to the city. There, I also met many graduate students from across the Columbia schools, who had gone to excellent undergraduate colleges, and they all agreed with me that they were disappointed with the quality of their graduate programs. Programs such as TESOL was offered as a full-fleshed Master, attracting mostly non-English speaking people coming to America to learn how to teach English and are willing to pay a high cost to attend these ESL training programs with a Columbia name on their diploma.

It was a taste of real life, though bittersweet. When you are put in that situation, you need to turn the table around. I figured out about this school in a semester, and learned to choose well after that. I had some of the best education policy classes with the best professors at Teachers College; they were passionate about the taught subjects, and that could be felt in the classroom. Yet, I also survived through some of the worst courses there with well-known professors. At the time, research opportunities were scarce to Master's students, and even if I was chosen for one of the teaching assistantship after my first year in the Master's program, they could not let me in because the teaching assistantships were reserved to PhD students, who craved for money to survive there. Their facilities and growing opportunities for students were left much to desire.

I found an opportunity to work at Butler Library, Columbia's main general library where the undergraduate and graduate students at the school of arts and sciences go to do their research. It was necessary for me to earn some pocket money, little it was, and an opportunity to connect with the Columbia schools and made me feel like a part of Columbia, to have that pride, that sense that indeed, I was accepted into Columbia and I was a Columbia student, and one day, I would be among Columbia alumni. I loved libraries and that library was just so old, so beautiful, so wonderful, so central to the intellectual life at Columbia. I also utilized the SIPA library to get more books in public policy, things that were related to education and law and that interested me. Since Columbia was also a partner of NYU, I also used the NYU library in Washington Square now and then to just read and enjoy the million-dollar view that this library offered. I would walk in that neighborhood on afternoons, imagining that I was even an NYU student, so chic, so glamorous, while enjoying the confidence of getting accepted to one of the most competitive schools in the US as a Columbia student, and savored the opportunity to study at NYU's Bobst Library. I was a "guest," but it was nice to be a guest at that place, using that library and experiencing what NYU students experienced. Spending all the money you could, but having that unique opportunity was not something everyone could have. Yes, I was more of a Columbia central student at heart, and I did education policy, where law attracted me most. Then I also explored New York City and unique places like NYU that made up the fabrics of New York. I knew Times Square. I knew Hell's Kitchen. I knew 34th Street up to 42nd street, up to Columbus Circle and Central Park. I walked everywhere. I walked to the Mets, the Frick, museum of natural history and other museums of contemporary arts. Certainly, there were the imprint of the Rockefeller Family there too at the MoMas. And Morgan's Library. And the hospitals a bit further down before hitting Lower Manhattan. Days were spent just walking along South

Ferry, testing the ferry to see the Statue of Liberty. Who could imagine that experience was mine?

*

*   *

Back to New York City, I swiftly switched my plan to Callen Lorde Community Center, a very well-known clinical center in the city for working with transgender patients. I had to retake a medical exam again with them, but it was okay. I saw Lyon-Martin professionals back in San Francisco, and they transferred all my medical records to my New York Clinic.

Columbia offered coverage for any surgeries considered "medically necessary", and fortunately the basic bottom surgery was one of them. That was one of, if not the most important factor, that pushed me to only select some graduate schools over others. UPenn and Columbia were among them, and getting accepted to both meant I could carry out my dream & plan of fixing my medical condition. When I first arrived, the school's health office nonchalantly told me they did not know about this kind of insurance. I was the first person to inquire. I fully understood that probably the policy was new and people were not informed yet, but that still shocked me for a second. It was Columbia, and things like this were not known or predicted in advance by the health and insurance professional staff. I made frequent visits to different health policy people on campus to push the policies forward, and obtained a fat chunk of paperwork explaining the insurance policies regarding the issue. I made several additional appointments with the psychologists at school and at Callen Lorde, as well as the doctors at the health center, to obtain all the tests and certificates needed for the surgery. I also had to find out about the surgeons willing to perform this surgery for me within a year.

Nine months after careful discussions and negotiations with both the school and Aetna, my health insurance company, as well as with Callen Lorde, I finally got the approval. Despite the flush of paperwork and problems at the beginning, I received a generous offer from them from my platinum insurance plan. It would cost me the same to perform the surgery abroad without buying the insurance, but with this insurance policy, I could work with an in-network doctor in the US. I was lucky enough to have an appointment from my surgeon within only a 6-month wait in advance. The man from the insurance company speaking to me on the phone explained carefully all the steps I had to follow, which was simple actually, and after a year of legal and administrative work, I flew to Arizona in the winter break where my hospital was ready for my surgery. My term exams at school had all been taken; it was the only thing on my mind. So technically, I had to pay 8000-10000 dollars in total for my surgery. It was a deal.

While at Columbia, I also audited some French classes. One was with a professor in the graduate program, the other with a French boy coming from France. I admired the professor, because he graduated from Ecole Normale Supérieure, and the classes were designed for doctoral students in the French graduate program, so it was a great thing to study in that class. I had a chip on my shoulder— and made myself separate from other graduate students— which was a silly thing that a low self-esteemed me at that time could not figure out how to negotiate— negotiate between politeness and confidence. Yet, I felt that class was a match to the Columbia reputation, and had a good time studying French there. The Philosophy Building, where the French Department at Columbia was hosted, was stern, serene, and archaically comforting. I felt belonging there. The staircases, the early 20th century lift to the 2nd floor, were imbued with generations of French and Philosophy Columbia students. It was only a school, but at least a school with a history, and I was proud to take a taste of that. The other class was a conversation class with a French boy from France. The class was in Hamilton Building, which was nice and housed undergraduate classes and administration. The class itself was designed mostly for undergraduates, and some graduate students from non-French departments. Somehow I had this fascination for the French. I wanted to make friends with them. It was probably a Francophile thing, so naturally I wanted to make friends with this new boy coming from France and obviously did not know anything about me or the US, or so I thought. The guy was smart. Sometimes I thought we could be friends, but obviously I had to keep a distance because being friends with your teacher was not exactly something I should have done. Somehow I was still very, very conventional in that sense. Relationships were, and have always been, clear-cut to me, and I tried not to break what was beautiful, sacred as a school relationship. I still thought he was a friend, just a friend; imagining him as a boyfriend was possible, but was not very entertaining. At the same time, I wanted to tease him. Somehow it was this innate desire to conquer, to make a man like you that I had. And so that was how felt about him. I did not want to push it to a level where he would be infatuated with me, or that we would be in a relationship, then hurt each other. Just enough so we could be friends, a boy and girl relationship kind of friendship, mixed between friendship and affection and doubt for love of a person of the opposite sex. Somehow I had that desire, that feeling inside me that made me appear perhaps coquettish at times. Shy, reserved, but the kind of shyness and reservation to attract people of the opposite sex. It was already in me. Somehow I guessed he, very smart, shrewd and observant, saw something and was interested in knowing more about me too, but I shied away from getting to know him or letting him know me more. I did not want to break that relationship, that friendly sentiment I had for him, albeit at times, I thought I could try to make it more than that with him just to know how it would go.

Fortunately, I did not. He was a boy to be protected, and I did not want to hurt him. It was a smart decision anyhow. There was one confession that I wanted to make, but never had a chance to tell him. That time he saw me sitting alone on Low Steps, on a sunny day after the rain in spring at the end of the semester, it was staged. I wanted see him again to talk to him after the end of the semester, and let him know who I was. I had to communicate with the insurance staff at school about the health insurance policy, and was at a deadlock because they were very slow and seemingly unresponsive, acknowledging of the item for gender reassignment surgery when, even before my arrival, I had already read that it was covered under the insurance's policy. So instead of sending the email directly to her, I sent it first to him, knowing the possible confusion due to the email naming at school with our initials and a random number code. I did that deliberately. Feeling bad about it, I also sent the message intentionally erroneously to another person at school on the Staff. The staff responded politely, saying that it was mistakenly addressed. He did not. But I knew he read it. That I received a message inviting to an admissions conference to some business schools in France sometime later, when I never actually signed up for anything like that from anywhere, was a sign. And on that day, when I was sitting on that marble bench overlooking Columbia lawn and the library, empty-minded and just thinking about nothing but the simple silence of the moment, as usual- on those Tuesdays and Thursdays knowing that he had done teaching classes by then, and as I was ready to leave because, as usual, scanning around the school and not seeing him, I guessed he had already left or never noticed me, when I suddenly saw him upon leaving and walking towards the library. He was standing there, since when I did not know, looking at me in my direction, when I did not even know it. He was fixed like stone. I, startled but fluttering in my heart to see him again, knowing that he was watching me and confirmed that he knew and read that letter email, was happy. I did not want a confrontation, or pretended to be angry when I was not, chose the other path of the two ways leading to Butler Library. I turned my heads to see him; he was still standing there, obviously feeling a bit discomfited that someone he was watching, caught him in the act. Little did he know that I wanted him to just talk to me. I walked away so he would feel happy to leave, untroubled, unafraid. But I was glad that he knew me. He had always seemed so protected, so French. I wanted to see how he would react seeing that situation in life, and perhaps let him know the intricacy that he probably did not expect to know. That was the friendship that I wanted to give him. Perhaps it could have been better, but that was what I gave. I hope he forgives me if he ever reads these lines.

And I also met a German boy. His eyes laughed when they saw me: I had never seen such merriment in one's eyes before. He was kindest, gentlest, strong, and most jovial boy I had ever met. Or perhaps among them. And yet, he liked me. He liked me when I was in the midst of the "metamorphosis"- but he liked me and it showed. I guess I was already almost 6-9months into the hormone treatment; signs of physical changes were visible, and people could tell. He purposely, or accidentally called me a "she"--- when talking to a group of friends, in the most gentle, merry, casual way. I liked him too, but I suddenly thought about the boy I had left behind in France and waited to return to visit. The consideration was weighty: between taking on with the new relationship, testing it, trying it, and dishonoring what I found so true and authentic as what I felt with the one in France, versus saving this old passion, keeping it, and distancing myself from one of the best people I had ever met--- and contented myself to only be friends with him. I chose to be his friend. But it was without difficulty and repercussion. He thought I was into him too--- it was probably in the eyes--- my eyes spoke of wonder, confusion, admiration, timidity, and reservation, or perhaps a combination of all that when I was with him. And we could have been someone together. But I honored what was best in France for me. And off was the relationship.

I lost contact with him, because he unfriended me soon afterwards after finding out about that relationship I had reserved for someone else and refused to add me back as a friend when I initiated the conversation. It must have been heart-breaking and disappointing for him. The fortunate thing was that we did not do anything that could hurt our relationship; I just did not take it to the next level as people normally would do in that situation. The unfortunate thing was, I lost him. Probably. I always cherished him as a friend, a friend to be with, and it could have been good that way no matter what happened between us.

I had to navigate through numerous issues living in a graduate dorm. In retrospect, perhaps it was smarter to live alone—renting an apartment, a room even, where I could be completely independent.

That way I could calmly use my hormone replacement therapy, and move on to live my life, a real life as I wanted. I was too silly. It was hard to go beyond the graduate environment at that time when you were there, and perhaps thought little of the numerous opportunities out there in the real world— the opportunities and the real life that all situations could happen— as long as I chose them smartly. I did not care about other graduate students. They were friends to be friends with in graduate school, but I did not necessarily have that desire to socialize as some people did. They came with the intention to find someone to marry too— as happened in many cases with these graduate students. They were not as wholesome either. For once, it was close to school. Second, they offered the best discount to live near campus, or so I believed even though in reality, there were far more superior choices that living alone, mixing and mingling with other groups of people could have been vastly beneficial to me as well.

The most fun, and memorable incident was one related to the bathroom. I was only several months, perhaps during my first year of hormone replacement. My body was still not fully changed yet. I cut my hair short, instead of letting it go long. I already contacted the house administration and they let me use the female bathroom as well as rooming me as a female student. Everything was good, paper-wise. I had to be careful anyhow, because I did not want other female students, who still did not see me as a fully-fledged female yet, or knew about the situation, my situation— I was an expert at discretion--- to see & felt uncomfortable. It happened once, however. Obviously some Indian girl saw me in the bathroom; they identified the 4th floor, where I stayed, so it was most likely me. It was only early into the transition, and I did not dare to have long hair, or dress in female clothes yet. We received an email telling us that boys should use men's bathrooms, whereas girls should use female bathrooms. It was hilarious the panic that caused. Nobody identified me, or could see me. Probably it was when I left the female bathroom and they saw it. There was also a Taiwanese girl, who had short hair and acted a bit like a lesbian. They could have confused her for a man too, but I'd take it that they saw me and thought I was a boy using the female bathroom. It did not panic me, or scare me, or change how I used the bathroom. I already obtained consent from the housing administration, and acted discreetly when using the bathroom—getting up very early when no one saw me, leaving the bathroom quickly when no other girl could see me. I covered up everything, wrapping around my bust as girls normally would do. Nothing calamitous. Nothing extravagant. Yet, the matter was still raised when I was there. It helped however avoid situations where some boys, lazy to walk to the other side of the hallway to use their bathrooms (there was only one type of bathroom on each side of the hallway—inconveniently), so they took the opportunity to use the female bathrooms instead. It was convenient that way. I did not take it as a notice for me, because I was never a girl and had never been a girl, so it was mostly to address the boys to not use the girls' bathrooms. That was good. I kept going on doing my own sanitation as usual, but it was certainly something funny that happened when I was living there.

About a year and a half at Columbia, I finally got my approval and appointment for the general reassignment surgery, covered by my health insurance plan.

*

*   *

I dimly recognized myself in a hospital bed upon waking up. Midnight. Not a soul was around me. I faintly woke up recognizing my nimble body and the strange environment around me. Two days or so must have passed since the day I checked in the hospital, chatting a bit with the staff to appear sociable before getting on the surgical table. I remember trying to reassure them that everything would be okay, that I would be fine with the surgery. My doctor, Dr. Meltzer, known as one of the best surgeons in the nation, looked at me, sympathetic; his eyes were warm and comforting like Mr.

Potato's I saw on TV commercials; he knew what would happen, before telling me that I would drown to sleep slowly upon anesthesia. We already met once before that for a confirmation appointment, when I flew over from New York to see him in the morning and quickly flew back the same day for school. I was sure of this critical choice of my life.

I moved a bit in bed, but involuntarily incurred then an excruciating pain at the surgical wound down below my abdomen. My body was limpid. I could not move; I did not want to move, lest the agitation would kill me with pain. I was afraid of blood loss. I imagined horrid things at that moment--- Death. Death after your surgery. Death after waking up from your surgery. I felt calm and serene though, despite the throttling pain that was eating me up and the silent darkness of the night, sleeping alone in a silent bedroom that enveloped me entirely and reminded me of my midnight hunger and the tedium of illness. I heard nothing but my own agitation, the throttling pain, jumping like my heartbeat and reminding me of the major surgery I had just gone through. On one hand, it was relieving that the surgery was over; on the other, I was also so weary thinking about the long period of recovery ahead, but most imminently, it was the painful surgical injury. I realized I had a catheter on, and I could not even move or shake my head easily because each movement would incur the shocking nervous pain that shot through each and every of my sinews. Darkness with its full silence fell on me. The solitude, the emptiness of the night was so much to contain, elongating with each moment awake.

Amidst all the pain, I found out that the French boy I was in love with was on vacation with a girl he had known ever since I left- to Venice. Such was a perfect day. Such was life situation.

Suddenly, I wanted to see daylight so much. I wanted to feel the normality of a day, the normality of my healthy body. I had never been that sick for such a long time. I wanted to move around. I wanted to not think about anything, to be just me and the simple silence of the day, and yet, my brain was weaving up a thousand of ideas and petulant worries, schools, jobs, careers, and pains. It felt like exploding, and I did not like it. I did not want my brain to be slowly exploded because I was thinking too much when my body was sick. I just wanted to be completely present in the moment, but just could not because everything felt like they demanded an immediate answer. And it hurt. All my ideas jumbled up in my mind. I was exhausted. I stretched my arms to reach out for the painkillers on the bed table near me, the nervous pain stinging me down in the bottom where the surgical stiches were woven. I saw those red-dark- almost blackened stiches, and the metallic stench of blood made me nauseous. I reached out my hand to find a glass of water nearby, quailing the scorching thirst drying up my mouth, and immediately tried to fall asleep again after that gulp of water, hoping that it would help me forget about the dolorous pain. It did not. I intermittently woke up in the middle of the night, counting time, hoping to sleep and upon waking up, the pain would go away. It did not. I reluctantly woke up each day to get my meals, and often just reached out to the remote control and made my order quickly on the computer screen in front of me. So many functions, I hated how even using a remote control was difficult for me. I sipped a few spoons of food upon waking up and saw the food plate fortunately just by my bed, to get some nutrition for my feeble body, and quickly forced myself to fall asleep again.

How funny, because during that time, I thought of the broken relationship, the horrible revelation I found out about the French boy I met. I thought he waited for me. I thought we waited for each other. I tried to write him thousands of letters- no, perhaps just hundreds--- to keep contact and to keep him abreast of my life and maintain our long-distance relationship. I guess it was only an illusion, and yet, it was not. He certainly made it as if it was me he waited. So all these years, I was lied to? I was living in a lie without knowing it? I played that Lana Del Rey's song, Paradise, on repeat, because that dark Gothic gloom was just how I felt. Pain killed pain. I had a playlist of Lana Del Rey's songs that helped me while away the time and forget the pain which was eating me out. It was good to while away your time and at least kill the boredom and the awful silence reminding you of your suffering, hoping for a better day to come. At least I did not die. I thought of dying. The pain at some points during my consciousness was pungent; I even had blood loss from moving. A nurse came in. She wanted to unstitch the spot, gradually, and replaced a catheter of some sort that the surgeon put down there. I thought I could die. I had rather die when closing my eyes tightly could not fully dissimulate that pain, and the metallic, iron smell of blood reeking from the wound. I imagined what it was like for women on the same hospital beds, trying to push out their children and that they had a difficult carriage. The pain, the suffering, was just like that. They had said, the level of difficulty for the gender reassignment surgery was only a 3-4 on a scale of 10. Goodness. I could not imagine what it was like for someone on chemo therapy or other major surgeries. It must have been terrifying. We were all in the same situation--- or similar situation--- and it was not easy.

*

*   *

After a week or so, I could wake up more voluntarily and regained my appetite. I really liked cod and orange juice, and ordered them almost every meal. They were healthy choices to replenish the missing nutrition to heal my body. I felt like my body was a machine, to be fed and catered to nutritionally, waiting for its recuperation. I could also talk to the old Taiwanese nurse that came to care for me in the middle of the night, and starting to recognize the world around me more fully. After 2 weeks, my hospital got me discharged, and I soon flew back to New York, alone, afterwards. Flying from New York to Phoenix alone was okay; I got used to flying around by myself already. Going back home alone after a major surgery proved difficult. The catheter, which had to be attached carefully to my body all the time for hygienic need, fell off at some point moving long distance at the airport. The doctor told me how to change the catheter, but not in this situation. I went to a bathroom, feeling like fainting at times, because I was afraid of seeing blood and replacing this instrument was not the thing I wanted to do. Fortunately, I found out a way to make it work. I succeeded in hailing a cab to go back home upon reaching LaGuardia as if nothing had happened. I glided right back onto my bed, and slept for a long day. It was winter; the snow dripped its flurries outside in New York.

I made up my mind to get some food, and upon waking up, went to a Rite Aid a few blocks away to get my nutrition, some milk and snacks to get by. I could not eat. I could not cook. I did not want to eat or cook. It was a natural solution for me to get something to keep my body functioning for a few days.

The following week, I was able to go back to work. Manhattan was very snowy in January, cold, large, and windy, slashed with the worst snow storms it ever had for decades. I covered myself up fully with several layers of sweaters while having the catheter on underneath. I usually loved the cold, the winter, and the snow, but I hated New York and its bone-marring cold those days.

My mind was not fully engaged in the Master's thesis; the surgery was full on me. I had all the ideas though. All I had to do was write. It was not that bad.

Fortunately, those days were gone. A few months afterwards I soon regained spirits again. I had to deal with other problems, of course, that is life; but this one, the most onerous that I had to deal with for 24 years, was finally resolved. Just in time for graduation. The sensation of having crossed that barrier to complete the surgery that I wanted for all my life was so great.

I could not believe it. I had a virgina now. For me it was an affirmation of a woman. I did not want to be half of anything, let alone something biological as a woman or not. I embraced it as Venus embraced her birth standing on a giant scallop shell in Botticelli's Renaissance Painting. Yes, I had a virgina, like any other women. And perhaps it was not perfect, but I had a virgina and it was the best thing that could happen to me. All these years, living in shame, frustration, internal combat about who I was and how I appeared to others. It all completely ended for me, fully, completely, not just partially because of the hormone replacement. I had a virgina and that completed the perfect picture, the perfect self of a woman for me. I was proud of my virgina, even though it was probably just cosmetic, man-made as many would say. It was still a virgina, an affirmation of a woman. Some prefer to be boys; I was a girl and I was perfectly happy in being a girl and happy to have a female virgina, proud as Venus upon her Birth as a fully grown woman in spring. I was proud of my own body, no matter what they said, because that was the part that God could have given me, but let me find it on my own, to complete the girl that He created me.

*

*   *

There's a will, there's a way. If something is true to you, if you are strongly convinced about something, follow your guts and find your way. You will be infinitely happier by taking concrete action than by living and always wondering, "what would happen if...?" Yes, "if", "if", "if" is an easy word to say: to wish upon the stars. But those ifs come to naught if nothing is done. We have to be the active agents that change our own lives.

Circumstances are often the excuse; our perspectives offer the solution.

It is not a matter of being a woman or a man anymore for me. It is a matter of dignity. I am a woman, and am fully entitled to intrinsic rights of a woman.

I read it somewhere, probably from Victor Hugo, that "It is not life that is unfair; it is humans who are". I contemplated on this and found that perhaps indeed, life is fairly distributed to us all. We are all endowed with certain abilities, and attributed with certain problems. The important thing is then to accept that and confront who we really are, and that is not easy at all.

Chapter 5
First Few Years
Living as a Woman

Sure, the vaginoplasty was important. It did not, however, change how I perceived myself as a woman.

Looks certainly matters in life, at least for a woman. Yet, being a woman or a man is also about the choices one makes in life. Compliments from others can be encouraging, but living solely on validation from others will only hurt you in the long run, especially when circumstances change and public opinions can also change with time. You, on the other hand, will remain the same. Fighting for your own values is fighting for who you are through the test of time. As we mature, we also look at life more accurately; our circle of friends becomes smaller, but they are also the people we can trust. I had many friends from high school who were very intelligent for sure; I went to one of the top high schools in the country after all. The problem is, Vietnam is a small country; people are smart, but the world is large and if they sleep on the laurels, others will pass them. The Fall of South Vietnam led to an exodus of Southern Vietnamese people abroad. Reunification did not heal the wound embedded in history. The Southern Vietnamese never recognized the new communist government. For them, their country was fallen. They were stolen of their own South Vietnam. Many of those left with a generation of smart, hard-working, cultural and social baggages. The invasion of Northern Vietnamese from Hanoi only brought with them indoctrination--- the kind of intelligence not seen favorably for those who do not agree with them. A pluralistic society was what was missing in the post-war Vietnamese society. That alone was proof that intelligence, social identity was much larger and harder to identify, even within the Southern and Northern Vietnamese groups of people, let alone the larger international community. This thinking helps me stay away from the provincial look on competition. That also helps me see people for who they are by looking at how they handle the challenges in their lives. How do they deal with their problems? How do they deal with poverty? Do they go out there, get an education, seek an education to build their skills, become better, enhance their abilities, or complain about life and wait for others to come help them? I believe how people go about to achieve their independence defines who they really are.

Yet, what kind of work can you do given your circumstances, and do we really have a choice?

As a woman, your trap is your own womanhood. It may induce you to less ambitious goals, and use your beauty as a tool to make a career without having the capacity to look forward and see what you will be like when you no longer have it in its glorious days. Beauty is a privilege, but is also its demise. A beautiful woman has to mentally prepare herself from early on for the day she no longer has it. She needs to constantly cultivate her character so that beauty does not incite jealousy and hatred, but rather admiration and respect, and that is an art that not all women master well into their adulthood. When beauty causes animosity, it is no longer beauty for me.

I was not tempted by this trap. It was a lie for me getting bogged down into a position where my only asset was only my looks; I was no Grace Kelly or Audrey Hepburn or Vivien Leigh. I was aware of that. I wanted to become a good woman though, a good, respectable woman, and I realized how much self-cultivation was needed to aspire for that kind of true womanhood. What I find true in many circumstances, is that we can actively control our social outcomes by eliminating undesirable options, and instead directing our work towards something closer to our interests, choices that will carry better consequences in the long run and help you earn a living while keeping you away from less desirable ones. Something like pornography for example. Some people think that pornography is an easy trade. You get money for having sex, theoretically. Yet, it eliminates many brighter long-term career options that you can have. Let us not get into how your life choices have already been greatly restricted by choosing this profession, romantically, you will start wondering whether someone is sincere when they enter into a relationship with you. What kind of a person is he? What will be the future of your children when they learn of your past? Sociological studies on prostitutes from Japan and developed nations have shown that prostitution leads to negative long-term social and psychological effects on the prostituted women. Many could not find long-term durable partners, and suffer from a plethora of social, psychological and medical problems involved with sex trade, problems that are taken lightly by many, but carry consequences far exceeding their original calculations. It was clearly not a smart choice.

Eliminating poor choices is the first step to shaping the path to build one's life, one that can help you flourish as an individual and weather through the challenges of growing up in the multitude of directions available and tempting us in the real world. At least in my case. I could not do prostitution; I had too much self-respect for that. Realizing your values is a major step to achieving your goals.

Another technique is to close out certain bad options completely. Humans are driven by ideas. You cannot eliminate their ideas, but encourage them to choose smartly. And choosing smartly simply can mean eliminating poor choices in life entirely as if they never existed. That will help you follow choices that will lead somewhere brighter with better social outcomes for yourself and other people. Some people choose routinely poor choices, but that is how countries and people remain poor and destitute. It was like choosing a dress: you could choose any cheap, inexpensive, on-sale dress out there, because it looks good and "acceptable". But it was not what you wanted. Would you choose it anyways? Perhaps if you could choose something you really wanted, even though it was more expensive, but if it was what you wanted, the satisfaction return was much higher and certainly outweighing the compromised dress.

One of the best ways to explore oneself to fully grow as an independent individual is through entrepreneurship. One is forced to think actively and realize your own limits and potentials to succeed. It is wonderful to have that idea, that desire, that passion of an entrepreneur first to pave way for your life directions, while also realizing your shortcomings for self-perfection. Being an entrepreneur is a broadly defined term. A writer can also be an entrepreneur, though not very well compensated, so can an editor, a lawyer, a doctor, an architect, a shop owner. It is liberating. The challenge that comes with entrepreneurship comes from some major financial risks associated with it. It is the most important, and is usually what scares most people out of entrepreneurial endeavors. Yes, you need to have money to keep functioning, but it could simply be read as that: you only need enough money to keep functioning. That means you can accept working for no pay for a couple of months, accept losses and use that time for your own business.

I was aware of that and wanted to start being an entrepreneur too. It was not native in me or through my education. Life taught me however that it was the best form of work, the hardest, the most challenging, but the most rewarding and satisfying form of work. I saved a few thousand dollars during my work at HEC, a business school in Paris at the time, and devoted to freelance work. It was not an easy, or fun period, because you could decide to have nothing to do, as what happened to me very often. Finding clients. Finding clients. Finding clients. That was the repeated refrains for me. At times, it felt like my clients were actually my employers, and I was applying to be an employee at multiple companies and businesses. I had my savings to fall on though, and I wanted to use that experience for good, while working and getting things done. I wanted to simply write, edit books, and translation. It was the branch of easily accessible kind of work for me, because my work at HEC or the OECD or the Rectorat de Paris- the District Department of

Education in Paris- used heavily editing and language skills. I saw myself focusing on the work and how to make money from my work and concerned about the business, which was a more natural way to think about work & creation, than simply accepting tasks and responsibilities given to me. I never thought I could do more than that. I could do more than what was given to me. I could do what was not confided to me in the office. I could give any work I wanted a try. I had that liberty. I could do anything. My thoughts were mine. My ideas were mine. I was a fully grown person. I could think what a CEO might think. I could sweep the office, and take care of every tiny detail in the office because the office space was mine. I had never thought of that power that I naturally had, and no one had to give anything to me and that I had to wait to be fed with work. That word was dreadful---waiting. I hated waiting, let alone waiting on someone or waiting for someone to give me work. Figuring that out was a liberating thought that I had never reckoned earlier, out of sheer folly or innocence, and it was not easy. I realized how much we lived in an organized society, so organized that we accepted readily what the society imposed what it wanted on us without us able to protest. There were rules, but I had that liberty to work, to be rich, to use my brain and personal work in anything I wanted. In other eras, that was how we had so many writers, authors, poets, constructors, inventors. Why did I never see it before, I was at a loss to answer that question. Out of sheer stupidity and naiveté perhaps. I must be smarter. I must read beyond what the society told me to, discern wisely, and act wisely. That could only be the single way I could have to earn my own liberty, the liberty that God had given me as a free human.

I realized that I was doing exactly what I would normally do in an office by working as a freelancer. The only difference was that I was not paid for the time at work, and that could be problematic. But I had no obligation either. No one was to tell me what I had to do. No one could push me or give me projects without me accepting them. I had to do all that. I had to invent work for myself. I had to find sources of income. I had to find what was useful and what I could offer. Yet, in return, I got to choose. I could choose the work. I could choose not to work. I could choose to sharpen my skills in a plethora of areas that I wanted to know well. Somehow, used to the common conventional way of work imbued in conversations, that you had to find a job, you had to be "accepted" somewhere to get a job; that freedom was strange, liberating but strange to me. I never thought of work that way. I'd never thought that work could simply be what I wanted it to be. Work was what I created, not what was given to me. That power is exhausting, but is also liberating. It will require much intellectual power and time commitment to figure it out, but it is worth it.

On writing this book, I realized that under any circumstances, working at the office could be exactly the same at home, so why not applying the commitment and hard work I could give to an office to my own entrepreneurial projects? I had this pain that after devoting so much to a company, at the end of the day, they just let me go coldly. It was what happens when people work in an office, and they are happy to see that happen to someone, especially to those they do not know or dislike. And for those who like you, letting go was something hard, but not something they can do much about because they are in the same fragile situation. It is a sad, unspoken reality that no one tells you or teaches you at school. Or perhaps at most schools, they do not want to teach people the hard truth and the hard reality that will hit upon their own graduates.

It was a reality. It is a reality. Sure it is a lot of risks to do something on your own payroll. Yet the fear was assuaged when I realized I could survive on little. I am still young, and I love working. Work gives me sense to my life. I could learn much by throwing myself into entrepreneurship and set something up for the future and build my own life. I learn to figure out my directions, all the directions I can take to further my own personal development needed to grow. Nobody taught me that starting something on my own was a possibility, a dignified, challenging, respectable job. It was often looked down and lumped with unemployment, and it was a hard thing socially and financially to deal with. Nobody taught me how to cope with fear, uncertainty, and that is the weakness of an education.

Learn to deal with fear- that is an essential part of a good education. Yet, that power, that liberty of work was unknown to me, and was a thirst I yearned for to gain an independent life built upon meaningful and productive work. Having choices is critical. Seeing choices and opportunities is just as important as the first steps to have them. I confronted my own smallness, the barrenness, the emptiness on my hands, but the wealth that ideas could afford me to build a better life- -- my own life.

So why not now? Why not start at this moment, this second, this instant? If you cannot find a good reason, then you know it is time to start. Do not wait. Waiting is useless. Patience comes with good things, but waiting too long will just kill the fish. Do not let it slip. Seize the moment. Get your work done. Fulfill what your heart wants to tell you. Listen to your heart and go in that direction as soon as you can. Yes, the road is scary. Yes, uncertainty is fearsome. But that is the purpose of getting a higher education after all: one needs to feel confident enough to tape the unknown, the lesser known in life, and explore the possibilities that mankind has always wanted to explore. That is the excitement of life after all, to know that we still do not know everything, and that there are possibilities of what awaits us ahead, given and reserved to be discovered for us by God.

When they wanted to kick you out because they felt you were competing against them, they just did. When they did, there was no appreciation, or something phony because they saw themselves too and that it was too often a scene that it became banal in the corporate world. Of course it is a lot of work and the learning curve is steep when going out there, deciding what work you could give in exchange for the concrete time you consecrate to your work, but the opportunities are also larger because you have now the ability to create work and create more work when you have free time on your hand. It is rough balancing between earning money and holding on to your ideals, plus figuring out the meaning of life, but I feel really satisfied with my work and the pressure I put on for myself. Obviously if you are satisfied with your current post at a company or an institution, I do not see why you should leave. We need talented people to keep good institutions alive. Plus when you do not know what to do and have to put food on the dinner table for your family, it becomes a natural choice. You are just as strong and respectable working there. At 28, however, I had this desire to test this world out and take the risks to grow fully, and I paid for that, but I grew from that experience and I could slowly define my life direction by pursuing what mattered most to me. I was weak. I was meek. But I had to be independent. I had to go out there and earn my own living. I had to survive. I did not want to die yet. Dying felt like a failure at something I could do, and still felt like having so much still to do to complete my missions here on earth. I find myself more complete as a person, a woman, when I can deliberately go out there and define my own path.

We can wear many hats, but there is only one that fits us the most doing just that. Many people have pursued careers out of complacence, only to regret it later on when they retire. They wish they had started something they really loved to do. It is a privilege to do what one loves for sure, but I find the regret similar to that of a transwoman who waits till she gets older before transitioning. The stakes can be high, but they can be higher when you grow old and realize that time cannot be taken back to relive again your own dreams. Figuring out what you want from life is critical in shaping your career direction, as time is a non-negligible element in your adult life.

It was not easy, and has never been easy, to figure out my own life, simply because my academic background was purely academic. Getting into the real world and finding my own place is a completely different thing. I headed for New York right after college; it was exciting and such a contrast to my little life in a small Ohio town. Manhattan. The famed Manhattan. The strangeness of this old city shoveled to my face a glazy cold stare of the reality: thousands of people whisked by carelessly in the subway down at Times Square, without a care of who I was. Yet, I learned to grapple with that change: crossing that fear is like crossing an imaginative bar: life goes on after that and it is liberating to know you can always live on and confront the new.

I did not want to be a careless woman; yet, I did not have an idea how to be a careful one. I could have worked in a bank- like that brief stint at Huntington National Bank I debuted as an unknown, witless intern. I could try to solve poverty. Psss... The idea seems absurd now thinking about it, knowing how my perspective on poverty was shaped by what I saw in real life. It was not sure if somebody was poor because they did not work, or because they worked hard and something did not go right. Earning life that way sounds good, but what's better than creating jobs to help yourself and help others? The top-down model that I saw at many international organizations, where theoretical macroeconomic policies were applied carelessly across nations, proved inefficient. In the end, it was those bureaucrats who earned the big chunks of the money and fatten their own pockets for their own wealth, without concrete alleviating solutions to the given problems. At the time, I also wanted to do journalism, writing, and law, working at UNESCO, the UN, and the World Bank. There are so many directions out there; one will lead to another but may also shun you from many others. I wanted to try them all, know them all, but I was too young to really know what the real games were out there and yet my ideas on them were vague. I was also afraid of stepping out into the real world. I excelled in academics, but would I fare well in real life? It felt like stepping over that fear, that imaginary but daunting fear: the fear might just be psychological after all.

Doors will never open unless you knock on them.

The hard work I had during my undergraduate years earned me a spot at Columbia. Whether it was big or not for others, it was for me. That was what I wanted and what I persistently worked at to accomplish. With this door opened, I could explore all the career choices I wanted to figure out my life better, especially in the field of education policy where I thought a tangible career. It served as the first stumbling block so I could work at UNESCO. At that time, I was dreamy, naïve, and did not know anything about international organizations. UNESCO was a fancy place to work in international education for me. Perhaps they had some good policy proposals, but not all of them, as I later found out in graduate school and in real-life practice. That idea though led me to an exploration of what had not previously broken known to me.

I had a large choice of graduate schools. I could also have gone to UPenn or King's College in London, where I was also accepted, but it would not make any difference, because Columbia felt like the rightest personal choice. I wanted to be a Columbia student and explore New York City and learn about everything I could about this luminous city "that never sleeps", something that Boston, Philadelphia, or London did not spark the same kind of excitement or cultural artefacts to me. London would be great, but it is not New York. People love Boston, but they are not me to know what I wanted. Boston seems beautiful and romantic. It is the home of the revered Harvard after all. I imagined it must be so beautiful: men in white fedora hats and buttoned jackets strolling along the docks upon intellectual conversations. On a beautiful, sunny, dozy afternoon, students languishing on the pastures along the Charles River, where young college men rowed along the soft-set sweltry Bostonian sun. It was so beautiful, so much of a college town.

Fortunately, I wanted to live in real life. The allure of college already faded in me. I went to a very small school in a small town in Ohio. I loved it there, made some great friends and knew some excellent professors, and I loved the campus golden in crested fallen leaves in the fall. I had an excellent education. It felt more natural for me to follow this experience with something big, something crowded, something amazing, careless, competitive, crazy, fearsome, and yet worthwhile, something like New York. I was glad I got in Columbia exactly because it was a fraction of that New York.

Columbia may have disappointed me, but New York did not. It was real life. It was the constant exposure to new ideas and festooning life created in that moveable feast that gave me its synergy, its peace, its quiet, its abundance and undefined sense of life. It was real life.

*

*   *

After grad school, I flew back to Paris to arrange some personal matters, and worked as an intern in a law office in the city. It was a great opportunity for me to learn and do work in tax law, French lax law specifically, something I had never known of before. I knew they taxed people enormously in France and that the welfare system was so big that many French people left the country exactly because of it, but I knew nothing about the magnitude of this system. Writing well in French was not easy for me at the time either. It was an opportunity to tailor my writing, and I would use it to leverage to other opportunities, at least in the capacity of a French lawyer.

It was rough, yet I grew so much because of it. I struggled to digest all the due diligence and tax documents that were sent to me. I read much on French law in the evening to catch up with the kids at Panthéon-Assas University, the French law school I was attending while working during the day. I had to stay longer than I expected in the office to catch up with the work. My supervising lawyer was a good, kind gentleman. He had a low, guttural voice, with deep-set eyes, and hair combed à la James Dean. He just started his own independent law office, everything was still nascent and I received a lot of mentoring from him. I realized the strenuous work as a tax attorney after a few months, but I also identified clearly what I had to do independently at home before I could handle complex legal tasks in a competitive law firm.

Right after the legal internship, I began teaching English at some local public schools in Paris. The opportunity came so suddenly to me after some posting. It was the TAPIF program that American students had in the US. I was selected then to fill in one of their vacancies, and by being on the spot at that moment, I was placed in the region where I lived.

I found fulfillment in this work. The kids were wonderful. Teaching a foreign language was like teaching music lessons when the kids could not understand the music well. I was in charge of 12 classes, giving them individual 30-50-minute sessions each. My kids were of all shapes and sizes: some were clearly eager about learning the language and working with me; some showed evident disparagement and discontent. It was such a ride, but I loved it though. I loved those big eyes looking at me each time I told them something; I loved the eagerness, the willingness to learn, the chitchat among them, their laughs, their frustration, or even their protests of disobedience. I loved them, even though at times they could be unruly. My schools were well-kept, and pictures by the children ran along the corridor every day I went to work. I fell so blessed teaching these children. Maybe I would not be able to do it now, because the pay was very low for an English teacher in France, and I had many other things I wanted to do, but when I retire in the future, I really do not see why teaching would not be a great option for me. I had the experience to know what I really liked there.

Then the OECD. I applied for some internships through the Assas-Panthéon University's career site, the law school I was enrolled in, and was selected for an editorial internship with the organization. Each opportunity was gained from succeeding at previous ones, and I always had to prove myself during the entire time. But I loved each of the work I did. I learned much about working at international organizations while at the OECD, whose work and whose people I had not the slightest inkling of, but I had it and it was informative. I interned as an editor at the organization at the time. Editorial could be tedious for many; it was not for me. I loved reading various research publications by the organization. I had the opportunity to work with some diligent, smart women, and that was wonderful. Some people were there because of the high pay, or the lack of job opportunities out there, but if you do not enjoy what you do, you will start feeling like a cog in the wheel, wheeled and pushed around by other people, and that is not an easy feeling with the competition and internal conflicts at these competitive organizations.

My career choices were shaped much more with each option tested and pursued diligently. I met many great obstacles along the way, obviously, but eventually, they helped build the first stumbling blocks so I could narrow down my career path better. It was much work, and it was rough. Yet, I found joy in the process of working and building my life through these trials. I felt more enabled. I am beyond this woman who achieves little but from her looks. I am beyond this woman who says she is independent, but does not know how to be independent; that she is free, but does not have the courage to create something of value on her own; or is equal, but does not have the skills, the drive, the competitiveness, the quality to rub herself against the best equally. And above all, the courage to find who she is, what she is most passionate about, to really work enthusiastically and serve as a role model for others, because if you try, you can always find something enjoyable about each profession you are in and infuse that passion in others.

I value highly professionalism and self-discipline. I also learn to respect, and expect that from others. I love working and devoting myself seriously to serious and productive work, and also expect the same generally from them.

Obstacles at Work and Ways to Find Myself as a Woman at Work

When I worked at INSERM (French Institute of Health and Research) in their accounting department, I had to deal with a woman named Fanta- yes, Fanta- as in the name of the Coca-Cola's drink. That was how her parents named her. She was from Nigeria, and came to France through marriage to an African man with refugee French citizenship. I was open to the opportunities to work with people from different backgrounds and social horizons. I was naïve to think that I could learn more about the French public sector through this work while earning some money to go by. Accounting was simple: you have to be accurate and honest in work. I identified many inconsistencies in the accounting work she did, but Fanta was recalcitrant and did not want to admit that. She also had this ruffian attitude as if she wanted to snap when you talked to her. It was understandable: she was a refugee, gained citizenship through marriage, and anything wrong at work could cost her this job, albeit small. Learning to negotiate those relationships to not harm people unnecessarily, while not making a compromise on integrity, was a precious lesson for me with this case. Avoiding direct criticism of her, I told her boss, Valérie, about it, so at least she was aware of the accounting work they handled at that organization, a scientific organization where exactitude and transparency were supposedly to be held high. Eventually what they did I did not know, but clearly the way they handled accounting matters in the office could be seen as fraud by taking money from different external organizations and charged them unscrupulous administrative fees at an exorbitant amount. It was outrageous, at least for me personally, having to work at a non-profit organization. I hope that my remark was useful, and that they would change the malpractice at the organization. I was also too naïve, too cavalier, too much of a Holden Caulfield debuting in the world of adults, to see all the dirty secrets it holds. Yet, I refused to compromise my values. I realized that after all, the beauty that can keep me clean and happy is the beauty from the inside, and as a deserving child of God, or aspiring deserving child of God, I need to hold on to my intrinsic Catholic and Christian values.

No one would be happy having that kind of deceptive working ethics in the workplace, as least not for me. Culturally, it incensed a feeling of injustice and deception in the workplace, and that could never lead to a happy environment. Perhaps these people already stopped their education at the high school level, and that could be a reason why their career just plateaued there. Perhaps not, because I also worked as an accountant for a short while in college in Ohio too, and my supervisor there was smart and capable of doing so much more. She was diligent, careful, instructive, and she probably never went to college. It was definitely her attitude towards the career and work that commanded respect from others and made the workplace a decent place. She was a Christian accountant. "God bless your heart"- I remember what she told me when I left. The world is tough, but God will lead us through. We need to keep faith, save our heart and soul clean, and keep on working to become the best self we can be every day.

Competition

Competition is brutal, but it could be both a good and a bad thing, depending on how it is used. If you are an employer, competition could be desirable in the workplace, though that creates certain problems that have to be dealt with to ensure people can work their best and feel best at work.

The most brutal competition begins outside the organization. Do you feel afraid that you may lose because your company is not attracting enough talents? Many companies try to attract the best people, because they know well that their companies' existence depends on the quality of their human resources. I learned to discern people and choose those willing to commit, because once people are sincere with their work, we will collectively create something productive together. When that is not a possibility, which is pretty often in the workplace with different ideological conflicts, you can also learn to identify people's abilities and tailor your work with them.

If you are working for a business, you are not, usually, handling directly with the psychological risks associated with running the business, but your job depends on the success of the company and things can go in multiple directions from there. Competition can be wonderful, serving as a motivator to hone new the skills that can be advantageous for your future. Regardless of your positions, there are always opportunities for growth that you can negotiate to feel best at work. If you do not like a position, switch, because recognizing that competition is an intrinsic part of social interactions, at least in the workplace, is critical to develop your strategies for career development.

Yet, competition does not only come from the outside. It starts from the inside as well. At the business school where I worked, I had to deal with a senior employee woman who had been there for over 25 years. I was a young, naïve management newbie, and thought that everyone would work collaboratively with each other at the same institution. It was a business school, not a big law firm where you can expect fierce competition among colleagues. Yet, I soon realized that she treated me as a rival, because I was really young and got a role that many vied for. I got in contact with her for a project, and I did not know about the intricacy of workplace politics until I worked with her. Her voice was starchy, honey-sugared, with a sycophant undertone. She pretended to help me, but I saw it through how she used it as an opportunity to promote herself to her boss by including her in the emails when they had nothing to do with this person. Once, I saw her break the cabinet of a colleague, who was on maternity leave, to get all the documents for her work over the pretext that she was completing a task for her boss. I was annoyed at how someone could go that great length to prove their work, losing what it is like to be a decent human being to others. Especially for a woman of over 60 years old, that was disappointing. I guess it is the difficult thing about work, you have to prove your values while also being a good person. I tested her by sending her opinion for a project to several people, without telling them the author, and they all concurred with me that the contribution was not that valuable.

Since her office was next to mine, I played once on my computer the word "pretentious", loud enough she could hear it. It was a crisp, loud sound from my room. The woman, who normally talked loudly on the phone and definitely heard me speaking on the phone in my office, also heard the music intended for her this time. If she agreed too that she was pretentious, then she would change it for the better. If not, it was just a sound.

The woman changed her attitude after that, at least toward me.

I know competition is normal, inside and outside the workplace, but overdoing it could be really bad, especially to people working in the same office. I was disappointed, because I thought a woman of her age would be exemplary in her manners towards others. I played the scenario and imagined how I would behave in front of future talented young colleagues, someone better than me. It would be difficult for sure, but age also comes with maturity, and you can make it go in your favor. If you do not want that, prove that you are the best by doing best what you can do early on. Choose a career that you love, because that is only when you can beat out most competition.

I have worked with many elder women before. They were respectful of others, and were such wonderful good people and I respected them greatly. They were happy in their jobs, and did not seek out opportunities to promote themselves that overtly. They showed their maturity through work. I guess this is the hard fact about life. We have to compete at times, if not most of the time, but we want to compete fairly and be fair, kind, decent human beings after all in the process. Sure, competition is normal, but you can channel it into collaboration, and use it as your motivation to work best at your tasks. People are born with different natural abilities; the point is to develop the best of our abilities and avoid hurting ourselves and others because of competition, especially in the workplace where we all have to deal with many sources of stress and we all strive to become our best. I find it useful to let the circumstances guide me in taking the appropriate action.

Or maybe she was scared. She was scared of losing. She was overly ambitious and wanted to rise and do more than what she could chew. But by doing that, she already failed as a respectable senior woman working at that company.

Enjoy the ride

I like to study people who have succeeded in their careers to a certain degree, and come up with a few observations about them.

Starting a business does not have to be that intimidating. People can begin in pretty much anything: beer delivery, wine delivery, pizza delivery. I guess it depends on the level of ambition in each entrepreneur, and though I may not necessarily consider the idea as formidable, what I observed about successful people was that they worked diligently to keep their business running. If it is honest work, honest investment, and it is not anything morally or legally wrong or hurts anyone other than their competitors, I do not see any reason why anyone has a reason to stop them. People can at least start growing their business, refine their ideas and do something better, with the increasing level of expertise they have. I knew someone from college who started a wine delivery service in New York City and became very successful, financially, from it. It was simple: wine delivery, with customized cocktail recipes for their clients. We could all do it, but he was a patient, hard-working man and he dared to get into the business. What happened after that to maintain his competitiveness was up to him, but at least he dared to start.

What is fascinating though, is that businesses and ideas can evolve, and you get to select and adapt to the situation. Like writing this book. There were things I wanted to share with people at the beginning about transgender issues, but eventually while writing it, there were bigger issues, such as being a woman, independence, and the woman's role in the society with both men and women that I deemed necessary to address. Feminism has gone downhill over the past 20-30 years, not having a clear boundary on what is right and wrong in relationships, some of whom have even started twisting stories to revenge on the men they hate by shoveling all the miseries they have in life. What I find disturbing is when they start making money off that, creating more and more of these programs and clubs at school. Something meant to be good, liberating women and their roles in the society, turned out to be a territory where it is about anything but equality. Work can be exciting in that sense: you draw from life experiences to refine your work and address new problems along the way.

Explore

This may ring true more to young people in their 20s, but explore as many options as you can in your chosen fields. One often finds a plethora of opportunities for growth by exploring deeper into the various niches of their industries. In education and law for example, find myself positively engulfed in a set of careers. I can work in legal education, clerkships, US Supreme Court, PhDs in law, or even paralegal. There are thousands of good choices out there. I find it important to not panic, and keep an open mind to opportunities.

The important point is to have a clear career direction in mind to guide you on a specific trajectory. The legal profession is special in that it has evolved from a practice-based discipline you could learn after college into a trained profession, which requires a degree and passing the bar exam to ensure the quality of the work. Study through practice if you can before going to law schools, or do both at the same time as what I did, if you consider going on this direction. Even if you may not become a law professor at a well-known school, you will still be able to pursue different careers in the field to eventually obtain your objectives. All the experiences will really shape you in your work and think about people, and with education, you can do so much more with the skills acquired.

Having something unique about yourself is obviously necessary to win in any competition. I find nothing more uplifting and truer than being yourself. You can have the best diplomas in the world, but eventually it is your character and knowing how to use the skills that will help you succeed. Integrity, work ethics, personality, likability, values that can be cultivated through serious hard work at your 4-year degree. Ability is what can be cultivated and shaped through proper education. Two candidates can have the same diplomas, but as they may have different personal qualities, perspectives and outlook on certain issues can already decide who the winner will be.

We try to figure out the meaning of life, our lives, and it can be frustrating thinking about it. It is a sign of human intelligence to question yourself these existential matters. Moments like this can be frustrating, but I find it consoling to write. Writing is a useful therapy to help with sadness, anguish, and loss that we can feel at times. Especially when you are at a certain point in your life, looking for a job or debuting an entrepreneurial project, this realization can come at you hard. You want to figure out a way to earn money, and yet, you have to confront so many barriers that stop you from getting there. It is not easy. Writing will help you flow all that sadness inside you onto the paper. If you want to keep a journal, go ahead and do it. I have been writing journals almost daily for almost 10 years, and it certainly has helped me much in relieving my thoughts. I explore deeper into my own psyche, my own life, and seek a solution from writing. Sometimes, writing is wonderful because you get to confront your own intellectual ability, your experience, and you seek to find and consider many options out there. That will help you refine your thoughts and your own life options. Just let go of your frustration by writing in a notebook. Remember that eventually, you have the right to keep your journal secret. No one else can read it but you. Have a password to protect it so you can protect your own privacy.

To minimize the risks associated with entrepreneurship, I find it useful to keep myself in check of all my projects by having a clear notebook of objectives that I want to accomplish every day. This helps with building discipline for everything in life, not just work.

Define your own paths- Choose what is yours

In traveling, for example, many people would travel to big cities-Paris, London, Barcelona, Amsterdam, Moscow, and other big cities abroad, showering us with lovely photos of exotic locations and exotic cuisines. It can instigate a sense of smallness, and jealousy in us at times, but know that many of those glittering vacation photos do not reflect correctly how people feel in real life. Plus, there is a learning curve for everything, including travel; people might have never been to those places before and wished to explore them. Shut them out however if they bother you. Do what you want instead. I love France, and that is all that matters to me. International travels are fun for sure, but maybe I do not need them after all. I may or may not have the budget, but it does not matter because I thoroughly enjoy the quintessential, quaint quietude of the countryside, and that is all that matters to me. I often travel then to places that are easily accessible to me, where France is still France, the picturesque old towns, idyllic countryside with the Church domes atop somewhere, removed from the rushes of daily lives and from excessive human calculations, or simply the coastal beaches in Brittany. Life can be that simple for me, and I do again and again what I love to do.

Perhaps I do not have the opportunity to visit many places in the world, but that is okay because this is all I need. And even if I do not live in France, I can get access to the ocean everywhere in the world, where the beach is beautiful and calm. I do not have to travel too far to get what I want.

Along the way, I know life is hard, but I put my faith in God and follow Him to traverse the difficulties of living, the sense of life that is sometimes taken from me. I try to lead a simple life, and simplicity can help greatly in enjoying fully what you have in life.

*

*   *

The journey continues. Life goes on. Successes and failures happen constantly, but I realize that stumbling and being able to stand up, move on, be able to still hope in the midst of the dark days, is a powerful vision: the vision of hope. Espoir, as they say it in French. And that Espoir is very important, because without it, days would be so harsh and life would be devoid of meaning after all.

Maybe indeed, it is really just beginning for me, given the amount of schooling I received. I feel like it was only yesterday. As I grow up, I also appreciate time more, and work more and better consequently. I had to start everything from scratch like most people, I did not have any connection to get the things that I had. But I realized you could earn those contacts and the best of them through working and showing the best person you can be. I also find the career options are more open to me now than they were, say just a few years ago when I graduated from college. The doors will open when you start building the roads to get there.

Shakespeare wrote in one of his plays, "All the world's a stage, and all the men and women are merely players". You have to play well your role and be the best you can in your role. Each role requires a certain set of technical skills and personal qualities. A judge should place the highest emphasis on integrity, honesty, Justice and Truth. A professor needs to be knowledgeable in a field, and be the good role model for students with a thirst for knowledge and its power to help people discover their abilities themselves through learning. Sure, we might just be players in this game, but we want to play the best good people in our roles.

Chapter 6
Finding Your Values and What Clicks

*

*   *

STORY OF THE FARM- June 20, 2009

After my marriage, I moved to a secluded country in Bristol with my husband. As he and I liked the simplicity of the countryside, we consequently built a plain house using our modest compensation from farming activities. Our wooded house lay high atop a hill, surrounded by the wind-swept prairie. Lush grass stretched far to the horizon, and I often took Mr. Rochester my husband outside after our dinner for a late afternoon walk. His eyes looked far away into the open land. The sky was clear; the majestic sun beamed out radiant lights, red and confirming, inspiring and exhilarating. The penetrating eyes were still Mr. Rochester's, and the warmth in his soft gaze kindled the love I had always devoted to him. Small gales swept over the open prairie, and my soul flew up there with the birds in the orange-deep sky. Our son lived with us too. We named him Darcy, because I loved Darcy in Pride and Prejudice.

We raised cows on the prairie. At first, we had two cows to fend for the necessities of our daily life. Each morning, I woke up at four, tiptoed outside to the barn, and silently laid down the bucket to milk the cows while they were gazing the yellow straws I collected with Darcy yesterday. Darcy had a particular liking for cow's milk, which I often mixed with strawberries grown in our back garden and other seasonal fruits (oh readers, my humble knowledge still allowed me to fortunately know that fruits and vegetables are good for my son's health). In our back garden, I grew Japanese cucumber, broccoli, green leaves, strawberries, and a small set of flowers that added different colors to my garden. On the left wing I grew different pansies; next to the pansies, I put several boxes of chrysanthemums and a few boxes of Sun Flowers which refreshed a corner when the sun set out in the morning. I liked Night Butterfly Flower most. Its violet wings fluttered silently in the corner of the garden, shy and timid. But when I got in, I felt the smoothness and the deep purple glowed, and arrested my attention. Purple is sad, like my soul- when my gaze looked far away in the flow of the unforeseeable circle of life.

My eyes captured the perimeter with which my lodging is surrounded. Darcy was riding a pony, the little pony cantered on leisurely when his master, raising his hand grasping a small branch, was playing the General Game. Oh my boy! I couldn't restrain the happiness to see my darling child there. He looked just like his father.

Darcy had got off the pony and laid down on the grass.

Darcy! – I cried- come inside and have the pecan pie momma has just made for you!

He sat up, looked to my direction, and waved his hands in my direction, motioned me to come to him. His smile is direct; it's always the joy of a mother seeing her little son growing up and is happy that it makes her so happy like that.

-Mom! Come here and eat with me! It's so breezy here!

My dear child! I was looking at him when a gush of wind swept over his hair and Rochester came up to him with his palms clasped together. There seemed to be something between those large palms, his smile was that of victory and satisfaction, the smile I always loved to see radiant on Rochester's lips.

My husband opened his hands, and fluttered away a hummingbird. The quick bird was flying, and I heard Darcy shouted out the shout of joy. The bird was free. Darcy loved the freedom of the people, of the animals around him. I shook my head with a happy smile when I brought the cakes to my dear husband and my beloved son. I felt like a girl again when the soft wind kissed my cheeks. My hair flew softly, and *my skirt rustled in the gale. Oh, a perfect family life it has always been my imagination! Now it has come true with Rochester and Darcy for me.*

Yes, that was my writing. My writing when I was 19. Right after my freshman year. I wanted to be a writer. I wanted to write a book. I wanted to start something in writing; I wanted to write well. And I wrote that piece, based on Jane Eyre.

I remind myself pretty often what matters to me in my life. Freedom is a word easy to say but harder to achieve in reality. Yet, if that is what you want, you need to reach out and fight for it.

I hope some of these will help you find out what works for you. Certainly, there is an abundance of advice you can find easily everywhere nowadays, but these are what I have concluded through my life so far.

Regardless of what happens in life, in order to preserve the little happiness in life, try to be simple. Simplicity is happiness. When I feel so charged, I take it off and start seeing things from the basics. I have to work hard, be sincere, honest, and open-minded to different opportunities and circumstances in life. Being simple helps you navigate through to arrive at something bigger and happier without feeling overwhelmed.

"No one owes you anything". This is a quote that I love. It is great because it helps you put into perspective about your own independence in life. Note also that you owe nothing to anyone. That is a powerful important message to know, especially in negotiating your own individual rights and what you are willing to give in the social contract.

We collectively also tend to work better as independent people willing to share something together, than forcing them to follow you when they too also have their own ideas. In the workplace, this could apply on multiple levels. On certain collaborative projects, you need to persuade people by offering the best ideas on the table, and have an influence on the final outcome. That requires a great deal of work, and also note that everyone wants to have a voice and will fight hard to have it heard. I learned this the hard way through a project. I presided a group meeting with people I had never met before and where everyone in the room was against me. I felt like they were the lions trying to bring me down. That was okay. I realized I followed rigidly my own agenda of how the meeting should progress, and it was a very poor idea. Real life does not usually happen that way, and it is okay. You need to be flexible enough to handle different situations and fight for your points. In my case, fortunately, it was only an organizational mishap. If I had a chance, I would get to know people, their work, their personalities, so the conversation could be more enriched and fluid the next time.

Keep fighting for what you believe in, and do not let the noise trouble you. People keep saying this, and I cannot say enough how important it is to have your own perspective on things, by evaluating rigorously what is right and just before making your decision to not waste your time. My game is in education and law, and I try to stick to it to make an impact.

Discipline. Jim Rohn, American entrepreneur and motivational speaker, once said: "Discipline is the bridge between goals and accomplishment".

Nothing is truer that the power of discipline to pursue your projects well and earn the satisfaction of accomplishment. It takes a lot of time. Even getting up daily at 6am and going to bed at 12am takes a lot of practice, and is not always easy, especially in the winter when the weather is cold and you just want to sink in your pillows and get warm under the cotton blanket. I sleep 7-8 hours though on those days when there is no rush.

When you are disciplined, you have a better appreciation of your time. That is critical to creating your own self-worth.

Concentration. I find it best to combine the two together in my work by having a planner. People have different methods to keep them active and on schedule, but I find it very useful to budget a day concretely with different projects on a fixed schedule. There are 24 hours a day, how you distribute your work throughout the day decides whether you can get your work done or not.

Explore. We are bored when we do not know what to do in life. You need to try working at different projects, studying, honing different skills, and find out things you like to do to avoid the feeling of emptiness and lack of direction. For me, I stick to my own career in education and law because I care most about them and they help me cultivate who I am as a person and what I can contribute to this world. That does not exclude socialization, but eventually, socialization is the gathering of people with similar interests, so you still have to branch out and find out what you are interested in anyhow.

Build Healthy Habits. I love sleeping naked, with the windows open. I am a dreamy and romantic person, and I am proud of it. I always want to keep my heart young and happy, and that is critical with me. This could be a strange habit to many people, but it is indeed very relaxing. You also sleep better, deeper by sleeping naked. Studies have shown that it could also be very beneficial to your health. I like watching outside the windows, where opens a garden with trees early in the morning after waking up from a good night sleep. Depending on where you live, it could be great to have some sunshine leaking into the room and your body early in the morning. It can be a wonderful feeling. Adding some quirky ideas like this now and then in your life can make it less tedious in the continuum of habitudes.

That habit can also come from dressing. Being women, we generally like to pay a little bit more attention to our looks than boys, but choosing the right outfit that corresponds to your personality can be quite a process. What is your style? Many young women do not have enough guidance on dressing and can fall for sleazy, easy way of wearing clothes. That can be both costly and inefficient in creating their personal style and image in the long run.

For me, personally, I love timeless pieces of clothing. I can use them all year round, and they always look nice and appropriate while saving a great deal of money. I imagine that there are pieces you only want to wear once or twice for special occasions, but for most others, I am happy with comfortable, snuggly, easy to blend in yet also characteristic clothing.

Black, blue navy wool pencil skirts and conservative dresses are my favorite. I have accumulated some pieces that are simple, elegant, and classic, in black and white, and some mono-colors in my wardrobe. Certainly, you have to stick to certain pieces of clothing to see how you like them in the long run, and test the frequency you may want to wear them. That helps a lot in investing in the appropriate clothing items and resist the temptation to buy new pieces that come in every new season.

In daily wear, I also tend to choose items that can go well in a professional setting. They could be for professional reasons at different levels, according to the audiences I may interact with. That way the wardrobe is diverse and suited for different occasions, while maintaining the quality and variety you want to keep. As a professional, I tend to choose something that is quick and yet elegant. That helps me a lot every day in selecting the right outfit without spending too much time in the process. You can spend time then to care about other things in your daily life.

Guilt about earning money

I know. It sounds ridiculous, but I sort of belong to this group so I know how it feels. My approach is to change your concept about money and charity. Money is what you earn for your work, the fruit of your labor. You deserve it when you can earn it by being productive. People also need to work to deserve their own existence and happiness in life. Sure, your parents may probably leave you with some money too, and that belongs to you because they have worked hard to save it for you. Privilege comes with responsibilities, work hard away at something that is meaningful, creating jobs and opportunities for others because many people have found that uplifting when they have money inherited from parents for example. Time is powerful in that with money, if you do not know what to do with it, it will just be money. You will be infinitely happier when you can use your money wisely. That is why it is important to find that one thing you are truly passionate about in life, so you do not have to get pushed around by the myriad of things out there.

Who you are now will determine everything you will be in the future. Who do you want to be? Just imagine a world without anyone, and you are the only person on Earth. What would you do in that situation?

That is my question to help me refine what I can bring to the table. Perhaps you would take care of yourself, i.e. food and hygiene, first. But perhaps you can be grateful then, because there are already people like that dedicated to this work in the society. Your role is to contribute something in exchange. That helps look at work in a more accurate viewpoint, in terms of contribution, rather than the benefits one can get without working.

Chapter 7
Children and a childfree lifestyle

*

*　　*

W hat is the meaning of life?

Some people find happiness in children. Yet, children come with costs: money to nourish them, educate them, send them to schools, afford them decent clothing, take them to several vacations a year, and so many other expenses such as medical bills. Far down the road, college is looming, as children need at least a college degree to find decent employment nowadays.

Providing them with the best quality care requires much time, work, and money.

Children might indeed bring joy to many people, but perhaps it resides rather in the fact that they are working at building something that they love to do, and that gives them a sense of meaning to their lives. Parenting well is the most difficult job in the world. It is the job of a caregiver, an educator, a builder, a motivator, a doctor, an engineer, an architect, a friend and a manager, and many more, all combined. Perhaps after all, people are looking for a kind of work that fulfills them the most. Generational transmission also depends on what people actually have.

That is wonderful. If children are for you and you are willing to commit to giving them the best education, the best lives possible, it is certainly a positive thing. In many parts of the world, having children is simply a biological urge. People really just make children without thinking of the consequences for them and their children as a result. This is detrimental, when the families cannot afford the lives of their children and shape them in positive ways, and expect the society to handle the work for them. On a large scale, that would be problematic for the society as we know it today.

Children are great, but they do not necessarily mean everything. Exploring the world of work gives me a sense to spend my life productively and enjoy life without having children in the picture. That exploratory process takes time, and is work itself.

I feel more fulfilled as a woman with work. I grow with my work and with the emotional reservoir in me as a woman, as I discover more and more every day the richness I can give to the world.

Being a mother can be a fulfilling experience for many women.

Perhaps at some point I'd like to become a mother too, but I only want to become a mother when I am more financially stable, and I can only do that by working and guaranteeing that I will be able to secure a good life for them. Given the world population now, I think it might even be fair to adopt. Obviously, in adoption, you have to choose carefully, because you do not want to encourage certain groups of people to keep on making children and expect them to be adopted. Adoption has also become a service nowadays where people can make millions of dollars from running the business.

Born transgender, I gradually find it a blessing to not be able to conceive children on my own. Even if I could, I do not think I would want to make any children either. Life is ridden with dangers and hardships, and there are so many children who need more care to grow properly. Those are the ones that can receive love and care, especially in the Western world where the European-descent population is dwindling. Most parents in the Western society and some Asian economies go to work every day and do not have time to take care of their children. That can leave a door for opportunity to channel your love for children while resolving certain contemporary issues in the West.

I taught English at some elementary schools in France in early 2016. The kids were warm and welcome, and even in classes where they were unruly and disobedient of me, I still loved them. Teaching English was not easy for sure, but it was satisfying in terms of interaction with children and the future you can bring them. There are careers that you can have if you love children and share your love with them, without having to make more people on Earth.

Life is beautiful, but it is beautiful because you try to make it that way. It is a bag of mixed beans: you have to discern the good from the bad, and the task is not always easy.

Many young women downplay the responsibilities of motherhood until they have children and confront the true reality of raising a child. It is difficult to become a mother. Laboring is only the beginning. Nourishing and educating children is the long-term investment that requires much money and time investment for the children to grow up decently. The courage and the time committed to be a good mother, a great mother, and an excellent mother respectively, can be immense.

At 28, I still found myself relatively young for children. My energy could be put elsewhere, personal development, and a career that matters to me in the long run before having a family or children for example. It could just be cultural. In many countries, boys and girls get married early in their twenties and decide to have children immediately after that. If they can afford their children's independence and protect them well, why not? Only that seems not to be the case in reality, when a father and a mother are still relatively young themselves. When a mother has a rich, fulfilled life experience, she will be able to share it more with her children, bond better with the father, learn to cooperate together to raise a healthy family. That seems to be the society we want to build in our culture.

At 31, I still felt the same. Life happens as I continue, with the opportunities, the joys, the mundaneness, the excitement, the encounters, , the quiet peace and reflection about life and God.

I met someone who was singing at church with me the other day. She had an American mother who was working at the UN. She told me that the Organization organized a campaign where they encouraged African women to get sterilized or use contraception in the past. Only 2% of them participated in this program.

A POINT ON OVERPOPULATION (AS OF 2018)

Can overpopulation be resolved? Will the world be a better place if we have fewer people?

The quality of any society is based on the quality of the people in the population. More people means more talents, but also more problems. Talents also need to be developed, and the surest way is through education. Talents are only one aspect of humans. Modern developed societies have moved away from the primitive model of multiple children to fewer, but higher quality care for each individual. That requires much money and time by the parents that having many children cannot afford.

Having studied and worked in international humanitarian work, what I find international organizations such as the OECD, UNESCO, UNICEF, and other UN affiliates, lacking in their address when it comes to education is the lack of focus on quality human development. Quality can only be ensured when the population is stable, and that work should be concentrated on building people as *individuals* rather than as *numbers*. The education policy staff knew that. We only need to make changes, to accept the reality of our population and really pursue policies that influence human behaviors to better tackle educational and demographic crises in the developing world.

Statistics and Analytics _____

African population in Africa alone has reached 1.216 billion in 2016 (World Bank, 2017), and is expected to rise to 2.5 billion by 2050.

Asian population: 4.436 billion (including China and India)

Caucasian population: 246.660 million.

The Japanese population was at 127 million (2015 census). Its aging population is a sign of demographic seniority, but it is also indicative of how much responsible Japanese people are about family planning. The Japanese government complains that they do not have enough people to work, but that speaks more from the Marxist perspective where people are counted as economic contributors, the driving workforce to toil and labor than about social cohesion and well-being of the citizens.

Our policies should learn to adapt to the demographic changes with time, till a point where it is healthy and people could live more comfortable lives. What scientists and demographists have observed is that poor people tend to have larger families, despite their higher likelihood to be dependent on social welfares and other aids. Policies should be adapted then to address appropriately. Perhaps countries whose population is too large now, should change their focus on the quality of life instead? We live in a connected world where there should be no prudery about this to help us improve our quality of life and the environment for all.

Certainly, some will say having children is a joy, though lots of work. I do not beg to differ. It is remarkable to remind them however, how hard it is to raise a child, how much it costs, how much liberty is taken away from them, the vacations, the free time, the heavy burdens, the emotional struggles, the physical exhaustion, they will have to go through. And in the end, their children will probably not appreciate it as much when they learn about this life. But it is an experience, a wonderful experience, but one cannot feel how wonderful it is without being responsible for it. One needs work to earn that happiness, but since that happiness involves the stakes of your own children, their lives, not yours, and you cannot have control over that aspect, that is a big decision after all.

Chapter 8
Faith & Death

BEING A CATHOLIC Faith

Being Catholic is great. Nobody tells you, but perhaps the soul really exists after all, because that is how we know something such as "instincts". Many a time I sensed that somebody was not right, a friend or a group of friends, but I held onto the relationships because I wanted to test them. I had a poor inkling that these people would leave me one day, because there was this invisible distance between us. Surely enough, one day, those relationships would end for various reasons. I find it normal and natural, because we all have those that we can connect with more. It is reassuring for me even, knowing that we have matured enough to select our friends better. "The Soul Selects Her Own Society" after all.

I have also grown so much a woman as a Catholic. I washed my filthy mouth to speak better and kinder as a Catholic. I learned to look at the world more accurately. We can all have eyes, but we may not always be able to see things clearly, things that are hidden from us, things that are right and wrong. I learned to trust in God to show me the way so I can cultivate myself a better person every day. I learned to fear less, and work hard to deserve what I have. The self-improvement happens organically with time with daily cultivation.

And being Catholic works perfectly well for me to understand transwomen, because the soul is the essential part of being a woman in the journey that God has given us after all.

Chapter 9
Real Women

A real woman learns the art of speaking.

She exercises diplomacy when she can be diplomatic. She is discerning in her thoughts and careful in her analysis. She understands that people can be changing, but that does not stop her from being sincere and faithful to others.

She does not yield in. She is stubborn, but is also open-minded enough to learn from life.

She apologizes for her faults, but also discerns rights and wrongs to fight for her values.

She dresses modestly. She cares more about the finer quality of things than their appearance. She understands that fast culture or anything acquired so easily, also often fades quickly with time.

She likes her femininity unequivocally. She loves working, because it gives meaning to her life.

She understands that money is important, but she channels her work so she can earn and use money productively. She does not become a slave to money to gain independence.

She learns not to hate, but she dares to challenge people who do her injustice.

She tries to cultivate her personality, but does not pretend to be saintly just for the sake of it.

She learns the art of elocution. She knows that speaking is an art, and she is still a student. She works hard to communicate better, articulate her ideas well to connect with people.

She is faithful and loving. She does not date a guy simply because of his looks. She dates him because she respects him, likes him for who he is, for the efforts he has made in his life and she appreciates him fully for that. She declines politely when she does not think he is the right match. She sees men as people, and not as sexual animals in relationships. She knows how feelings are so important to human beings. She offers friendship, and knows when to stop to not push the relationship to the dangerous border of love and friendship.

She loves reading. It teaches her moderation and self-measure, and reminds her that she needs to cultivate herself every day.

She respects men to not hurl hurtful words at them without reason. She is able to see them as sons of somebody, fathers of someone, or someone who's been hurt by life. She understands that men can sometimes hurt her, but she draws the line and teaches them appropriately.

She is not afraid to fight and compete in battles where she deems necessary.

She works hard to earn her own independence. She keeps her dignity and work ethics, and believes in God to guide her.

She cultivates herself constantly because she knows that she is imperfect, but she works towards the most perfect version of herself.

She is uncompromising. She holds her values high and will not let anyone break her easily, least of all her values.

She is not afraid of life. She works hard every day with a goal in mind and she will do everything to get there because she knows what she wants and will work hard learn much and do everything possible to win. She is not a quitter.

A real woman exists, because she learns, and relishes in the process of growing every day.

And sometimes...

Sometimes, I just want to be a woman, that's all. Nothing more. Just being a woman, curved up in my little corner, feeling safe, secure, protected, no dense conversations, ideas, thoughts, plans, careers, jobs, work, school, education, the world, poverty, hunger, scare, grammar... No nothing. Just a simple woman in the silence and solitude of myself, but warm, cared, and protected, hungry perhaps, but safe in silence and emptiness, away from it all, just me, being a woman.

Chapter 10
Communicate

Womanhood is also about communication— talking to other people, talking to men. Yes, I learned from other women to communicate, and communicate better as a woman. Cultivating manners is not easy; it takes practice, listening, and contemplating on perfecting this essential art form to live happily by speaking correctly and saying appropriately what you want to say.

A Harvard study in 2012 by Krupnick identifies differences between men and women. The research discusses principally on how men and women communicate differently in the classroom. In her study, *"Male students talked much longer in the predominant classroom circumstance: i.e., the situation in which the instructor is male and the majority of the students are male. The presence of female instructors apparently had an inspiring effect on female students. They spoke almost three times longer under instructors of their own sex than when they were in classes led by male instructors. This led us to speculate about the importance of same-sex role models."*

I find myself less inclined to talking when the instructor is female under certain circumstances. Perhaps it depends on the women you are interlocuting with. Some women tend to not have a very broad perspective on various issues and thus tend to cage us women into a small, narrower and safer way of thinking for women. I do not like that. I prefer working with smart women, who have already considered themselves as equal with men, and proved that through their work. You do not see the gender gap studying with them. They might not necessarily be my role model, but I learn greatly from them.

This study though sheds light on interesting points. Women tend to serve as peacemakers as they wait till everyone in the classroom has gotten the point before moving on. Men tend to keep on speaking in a competitive way. Women tend to interrupt mostly other females in a collaborative way, whereas men may interrupt each other competitively. The differences go on, but you see, the sex difference is already inherent in the way we communicate and talk to one another.

That could help us a lot in treating other people in real life. I learn to handle a conversation specifically with different people from different cultures and different communication styles. In a heated conversation, people may just talk, talk, and talk, so expecting a moderate and polite conversation all the time is not very realistic. But being polite in conversation is essential anyhow.

Learning to appreciate the differences between the sexes can really help you treat people more appropriately. Just as something is so inherent in us women, there are also something that is inherent in men. Men tend to spread their legs a lot when they sit. If you do not like that, let them know so they can be more mindful about that, but also understand that, it is masculine to sit in a certain manner. Just like us, a woman spreading her legs in public places does certainly not look very decently. Let men know that they also need to respect other people, but also let them be men, show their masculinity in the appropriate manner, the appropriate measure of the situation. They can be masculine; you can be feminine. We are complementary to each other after all. Forcing men to act like women is like forcing women to behave like men. When they are not natural, they will break.

The Art of Concession

Being an independent woman also means mastering the art of concession. Accept men for who they are. Accept them and their efforts to ask you out, flirt with you, dress up decently categorically on a date, try to please you, sing to you, pay you dinner on the first date even though he is broke. I think that is something.

This is a social phenomenon of our time to make fun of men for simple gestures of flirtation. This creates a medium for some women to profit from the solitude of men and women for gains other than love. Eventually, all would be hurt.

Susanne Venker, author of *The Alpha Women's Guide to Men and Marriage*, wrote, "*Every relationship requires a masculine and a feminine energy to thrive. If women want to find peace with men, they must find their feminine—that is where their real power lies. Being feminine isn't about being beautiful or svelte, or even about wearing high heels (although those things are nice). Being feminine is a state of mind. It's an attitude.*"

Sometimes it could be good to use our maternal love to look at men. Women are empowered with the power to forgive. You do not forgive all the time, because certainly there are things that are so important, so precious, so core and fundamental to our beliefs—such as fidelity — and we also teach by being firm, but we also learn how to work as well to maintain and nourish a relationship instead of stifling it. If it helps, I think it is useful to find photos of men you love to forgive and see how they have grown up over the years. I'll tell you, the mother instinct in you will tell you to treat them more appropriately.

Some men also told me they look for women who are mature and can understand them, and can converse with them on important intellectual subjects. Reading is an effective way to be cognizant about topics and converse with people.

Every woman is different. I am not here to philosophize about how womanhood should be for them, but there are certain things that I find working and can be addressed appropriately, and would like to discuss it so with other women.

Chapter 11
Love, Family & Relationships

L
ove is a funny thing. It comes when you do not expect it, and also leaves when you least expect it too.

I had one or two guys who had a crush on me at each grade school, but that was it. I found it fortunate since though I am a girl and it is normal for a straight guy to like a girl, as a transgender, my position put me in a difficult position. At least I had the feeling that other females of my age experienced. At the same time, I felt trapped, and did not really pursue any of those relationships.

I met someone that was the hallmark of real love for me when I first came to France. It was instantaneous. That moment he appeared, the whole world seemed to just disappear. Stood before me was him and him only. It was like that face you had been longing to see all your life, pre-life and pro-life perhaps, suddenly appeared before you, the face that corresponded exactly to every detail of the one you should meet in your entire life. Search no more. The heartbeat, the environment, everything...

We never really said we loved each other. I came back to the US to complete my studies after my junior year, and he seemed to pick up the signals and waited for me all those times.

I waited for him all those years. I hastened to finish schools and this crazy transgender thing I had to deal with, but it was probably too late.

After graduate school, I got contacted by someone from the UNESCO Office in Venice asking me for a letter of motivation for an internship in their office. I was very happy; it would have been a big step following my graduation from graduate school given the number of applications they received. And Venice... Who could give up on that? It was the city of love and Casanova, and Italy seemed an ideal place to be right after graduation...

I gave that up, because eventually Venice was nice, but it was not Paris. And Paris would mean nothing if it were not for him. I also did not want to be this career woman who gave up on something as sacred as love. Time had taught me I could live anywhere, just not in crazy places obviously. In fact, I had rather stayed in New York for a few years, or Washington, or San Francisco, or in the South that somehow I found charming. Venice was nice but I guess I did not need to live there after all.

I came back to France, found myself an apartment, then headed off immediately to his office. It was early in September, and Paris was grey and changing seasons. I had problems with him after seeing all the photos a girl he knew posted on her social media all these years. She could have just been a friend for him while she, on the other hand, probably wanted more and set up the situation that way. It was over the border though.

I walked into his office. He was surprised, but forced to remain casual. After some light conversations, he hastened to tell me that she was his girlfriend when I did not even ask. So he knew why I came. He probably lied because I reproached him much about it before that after the discovery, in writing, a few months before flying back to France, but I had my reasons. He was funny, kind, loving, intelligent, and sort of boyish, but also mature and considerate. That was why I loved him and that was also the reason why I suspected he lied to me. He wanted to play me. We were similar in many ways, in thinking about love and showing affection for each other and predicting what the other was thinking. Yet, this could have been real, and I would not know unless I got the truth. This is a thing that I do not understand about French boys and which makes it more difficult. They have a very different relationship with female friends than Americans do. As someone who is used to American standards of masculinity and social interactions, it was difficult for me to know how they really handle their relationships with the opposite sex. In fact, when I first came to France, I was surprised at the level of femininity among French guys. I thought some of them were gay even, but they were not. Obviously I fully support gay couples, but it was not right to fall in love with a gay guy when you were a straight female.

He could have lied, but that was exactly the reason why I came to find out. I had my moral constraint; I already told God and asked Him to let me go back to France to see him and ask things out clearly, for once. I had to keep my promise.

He invited me to his apartment, where he shared with this person. I thought it was an insult. It could have been an insult or a sincere invitation, depending on their actual relationships.

Eventually, I told him, "I will think about it," and walked out the room without saying any more words. It was a smart move because I did not like it either way. When I was walking out, he wanted to say something, but I walked away anyways.

I hated him, but I also strangely loved him. I wish he had told me it was all a lie, and that he loved me and we would be making love to each other right there in his office. I wish it were a lie...

I politely closed the door behind. It was his work office anyhow, and I saw no point in being too demonstrative. I should have crashed that door, should I not?

*

*   *

Every story is different. That was mine. Fortunately, I did not lose anything. Keeping myself whole was worth it not to get into trouble in unwanted relationships.

Love is tough. I have come to accept that being single is okay when you have not found someone who corresponds to that level of connection.

It is rough to be single, especially when you see people go out together in pairs. I find consolation in the fact that everything has to come naturally though. Relationships cannot be forced. That is what happened in more ancient times, and in primitive societies nowadays. People can get married for various reasons, but what I find enduring is that when the two people in the relationship are sincerely together. Otherwise they will end in a divorce, or as in the Asian culture, they live in pain for the rest of their lives.

For the moment, I love being single, the quietude, and the freedom I have to explore and fulfill my life. And guess what? I am free to go on dates!

My love story never stopped there. Indeed, the search for love is a long search, with interesting twists and stories.

Confessions of a Catholic Girl

He, the man, invokes the womanhood in me. He, a sacristan; I, a Church faithful member. His slender, tall body does not and will not hide his firm statue; one that evokes protection. He smiled, looking at me. I, pretending not to reply in a smile, kept a bold face and walked to the altar, but my heart was dancing a triumphal dance, and yet, warm and secure, the feeling of a woman feeling protected.

I am a girl with a history. I planned on telling him on our first date. Would it work?

He is a well-bred person, despite the unappreciated job he does. It does not matter to me. A job is a job. If I like him, and love him, that is where we can start building our future together.

This is what bothers me the most in dating. I was afraid men will turn away when they know about my history. Certainly I am prepared to face rejections, but I'd rather not face it directly or repeatedly when I can live happily without having to justify or bother myself with heart-wrenching itty-bitsy matters like explaining who I am to others. I do not have to let people know everything about me, and certainly, before entering into any real relationship, my role is to break it to the one somehow about who I was, because I want him to be comfortable and know the truth about the being he wants to be with. Maybe writing this book will do. They need to do research about the woman they go out first before going out with her, in a committed relationship. That relationship, is it too hard? Sometimes I just want to be myself. I do not want to explain anything, and maybe that is the right posture. The man who wants to be in a serious relationship with me can read, and find out, and judge for himself, whether I am a deserving woman for him or not.

I guess I am happy to be a Catholic. Seeing what is happening out there, wife cheating on husband for the brother in law, and jokingly, wife having a lesbian affair with sister in law, I guess this world is sort of messed up. I wanted to join the Convent, but I heard of problems at monasteries, and the prospect of living with a bunch of women and their whinings all the time, plus their shrieky voice, just puts me off. I do not like being around so many women where the potential of exposing myself to the female problems when we are together is high. Not all these women are nice. I have contemplated on my quality as a sister. Maybe it is better to live it that way in real life than to join the Church. Many sisters at my local churches in the past were seemingly immature, and figuring out ways to live. They wanted to live, so they joined the Church. The eternal issue of cleanliness of the soul is present, whether you join the Church or not. I want to cultivate myself without becoming a sister and restricting myself to what people give me at Church.

Plus, I have feelings for men. Plus, there will be priests. And I am also not entirely sure how to feel around men. I feel pristine. I would feel pristine if I were to live in a Monastery. I do not know how to feel around men though. I had feelings for priests before. In fact, there was a great guy who chose to become priest that I knew of. He was such an intelligent boy, so smart, so brilliant. Somehow, he chose priesthood, probably for the same reasons as I chose to become pristine. Or, perhaps better, pure, clean, and Catholic. Anyways, he was so captivating, his voice energetic, engaging, warm, and sincere when he lectured on Sunday masses. He went on to become priest at one of the most, if not the most, prestigious Monasteries in the city. Perhaps I did not have that luxurious sexual want for him, but that was because I was a decent person and chose to respect people for their choices. I guess he was a great and decent person, and it would be wrong of me to lure him out of priesthood, to put doubt onto his mind, to tempt him out of his career choice, and to rob him of his pristineness. They gave me comfort, as I also felt how they felt at ease and enjoyed their masculine presence around me. Like with this professor I accidentally met in one of the work meetings where I used to be. It felt good to be next to him. It was like being with a male friend. And nothing was there to stop us from feeling good, warm, and safe around each other. I guess some priests still have that lingering presence of their masculinity with them too, but I tried to ignore any sign that could create problems to us and them by exploring the unexplorables, the deterred. With this priest, it was different. I guess I could be with him, as a female Church servant, a Convent Sister, so I could be around him and be with him to serve God and the Church's missions. That would be the end there of a complex, but not morally wrong relationship. I was afraid of nascent feelings between us, but these feelings did not feel that wrong, that bad after all. I am put off by the idea of an intimate relationship with him anyways, because we were supposed to be pure and good to each other in the Sacredness of God.

Such was my thought of a peaceful day working at Church, serving God. Was I expecting too much? Was I doing the unnecessary in life? Perhaps. In the end, the Church matters most to me though. Perhaps it is sinful indeed to even think about it after all. It is not easy, but it is important to save our thoughts from sins, isn't it?

Obviously I only love men when they are in the most difficult situations for me. I do not know why, but why can't I love some normal boys? I guess if that is the case, it will not be love anymore. Love is not easy. And loving a priest is the most difficult, but probably most akin to the love I can give and want to give. I want to give a pure love, receive a pure love, friendly, platonic, and yet caring and devoted love, to a man of God. That way we can both protect each other in the road ahead, our road toward Salvation and toward God. We are clean before God, and that is the friendship and relationship I want to keep with men. Why do we always have to be together? Why do men and women have to be together to feel good and safe? Why can't we be just pure friends for life? I saw the boys in them, the friends that I could have made when we were schoolchildren, loving, caring, and protecting each other. I also saw the potential platonic, priestly man and female relationship with them, but I had to stop that, because once they chose that profession, I did not want to trouble them with these thoughts. I do not least of all want to wake up the man in them. I want the pure part of them, nourish it, be with them, and we both could lead the local Church, be happy together as man and woman, and yet in our platonic relationship. Love and affection, but never vulgar as reaching copulation. No, that is too animalistic for me. I imagine we could stay in bed together, hold each other, safe, away from all the dirtiness, the mouth of the world, of all the craziness that this world could bring. But that was it. I want us to be together that way, serve the Church, and stay away from it all that we consider sinful, dirty, and secular. Where is the fine line between secular and cleanliness in a relationship? Yes, this is the love that I want. Perhaps I can never get it, and perhaps it is never realizable, but that is what I want, that is what I wanted. I was afraid I might hurt them for the profession that they choose, but I cannot help feeling that affection for them. I want to protect them too from this world, the fear, and the craziness of this world, but I do not want to create any social problems that they might not be able to handle either. Oh well, story of my life, always entangled mentally in these impossible relationships. Perhaps they were possible, and are possible to many, but as a Catholic woman, that struggle is real. I imagine some nuns have feelings for priests too. But the torment, the worry, the scrutiny and potential social punishment, is not easy to handle. Obviously, we care, and we do not want to create problems. We just have to be the most decent, reserved, and stay away from these open relationships, to protect people. I can get involved that way, keep myself clean by staying clean of wrongful relationships, and that is how I can contribute to the betterment of the world and what I do in life. It is not easy, but it is important to work and think of work that way. Protect people, and think of work in terms of normal personal human exchange. Help them. Participate in things that show you care and love them, but never awaken the man-woman love in them. If yes, know that it is just purely biological. Keep it pure and clean, and save us all from disgrace because of these relationships.

Why is it weird to many people? I feel maturity an asset before getting in an intimate relationship with a man.

I have to talk about my dream last night. It was such a dream. I felt perfectly satisfied with what happened.

Somehow I met a decently handsome, kind, mature, well-educated guy, of my stature, with short, pushed back, but well-groomed hair. He was also extremely polite, calm, mature, and wonderful. I felt so much at ease with him. I do not remember exactly how we met, but we were moving in together to an apartment, a comfortable, roomy, classic, with yellow, warm lights, and a pretty bed with thick, creamy white linen. In one of the scenes, I went to bed, and he slept next to me. He also vroomed around in a white Ferrari, and we vroomed together inside a Protestant Church Community. We went through the gate with our car, saw what we expected of the community, quiet, living to themselves, a bit shabby place, then quickly went out after observing what was interesting there. I felt so happy being around him and found it so perfect that somehow we were a thing, a married thing. At our home, he also showed me his knowledge of using some sort of home scent, which I did not use at my home because I thought the smell would be horrendous, but it smelled so good at his place, and such extravagant knowledge of the place. People said that did not matter, but it feels easy and comfortable around those who were born and raised in decency and wealth and comfort. It felt like that around him. Maybe I'd like to be around a rich boy after all, because then I would not have to feel awkward because of people analyzing me and my living habits and baffled by what I do, even though I lead a very simple life. At least I hope people could be a bit more understanding. Well, I guess I still have to live a simple life, be decent, be kind, and enjoy things without pretense. That way I can appreciate better what I have. Keep it low and decent, that is important. Anyways, the boy in the dream was accustomed to all that, and live as a normal guy with good hygiene and decency, so that made me comfortable. I hardly saw any guy like that nowadays, so it was such a break from all the mental problems I have right now with people and what they do. I guess in real life, I can accept whoever I have, and help lead us into a peaceful, warm, loving relationship like that. Also in the dream, in another scene, I also cooked dinner for us after roaming around. It was some sort of beef soup. I saw we ran out of ingredients or something, or that I have been using the serpentini pastas (torso-shaped noodles) so frequently recently, so I used the elongated pastas instead for a change. He was calm and nice in expressing his interest for the regular pastas, and that was what we did. I made him a bowlful of this curry beef stew, and obviously I guess it was good. Somehow my little brother was also there, and I also gave him a lot of beef stew to feed him.

Then rang. I woke up because the phone rang. Well, obviously I slept in a bit, because I did not want to get out of this dream with this wonderful boyfriend of mine and our happiness at home. Perhaps that was when I dreamt of the dinner with him and my brother.

Before that, it was only him and the Protestant themed dream subject. Goodness. I remember scrutinizing his face in the dream, and although I cannot recall it exactly now, it made me feel so warm and happy. His face was almost like that face of the boy I had a crush on when in high school. Unfortunately, the boy had a girlfriend, and it was sad for me. It was then that I realized the intelligence did not mean anything when it came to love.

I am happy that I dreamt about the boy. It showed me that I could move on, and dream myself with someone else already. It also showed me how I had no embarrassment about myself, and accepted myself fully as a woman subconsciously. That was a wonderful sign, because that was what all of this is about: accepting myself subconsciously without a doubt that I am a woman and my story is the story of a normal woman with her joys, her problems, her struggles, and her everything that makes her the woman that she is.

DEAR DIARY...

September 26, 2018

I almost forgot. Last night I dreamt of something beautiful. I dreamt of meeting this guy that I had a crush on in this dream. He was fit, kind, cheery, handsome, and looking intelligent. I think we met through a friend, and we had an interaction of some sort, which made me closer to him and thus liked him. Eventually I made the move and asked him to be my boyfriend. He said yes, or wrote me an endearing note, saying that he liked me too, right from the instant he met me, so he was glad that I asked him and obviously he would say yes. He invited me to come to a tutoring program he was running, and I could be teaching at the high school level there. How nerdy this dream was, but I felt that was so loving, so great that he was the head of that tutoring program. I said yes, I would be willing to teach the classes prépas there. He also revealed, obviously there was a confession note or personal inventory about him, that his mother was a TV superstar, he was connected to well-known people that I know, and that he himself went to ENS and all that, so that was why he was shy and difficult. I also went to a good school myself, so he could not have any reason to feel unequal about in that relationship with me. It was such a beautiful date that I could totally have in real life. And oh, I think he told me his name was Denchert, or Denfert. That makes me think of the Denfert-Rochereau Metro station, which makes it both funny and memorable that way.

*

*   *

I was lying on my bed, reading Hemingway's *The Moveable Feast* and realized how much affable Hemmingway was, how much of a young man, a boy in Paris he was when he wrote this book. All the details of an American in Paris, certainly evokes something lonely, unique, independent, and lovely about an American in Paris. I got instantly reminded of a lawyer, an American lawyer in Paris that I recently got acquainted with. He was a true embodiment of an American in Paris too, and I imagined how happy, how free he was an American making his way to this country, with the French culture he loved to explore.

Chapter 12
Conclusion

T his chapter is relevant to those who have ended their studies for a while, and find the necessity of schooling to advance their careers. I just want to shout out to you that, yes, it is possible.

There is still hope, as long as you don't lose it. Work away at everything and get it right because you do not have time and many opportunities from the beginning. Do a selection and get everything true to you from the start, because one accomplishment will lead to another.

Right after college, I just wanted to stop studying. But getting more education was necessary for me. I also needed a tranquil time for my transition too, so graduate school was an appropriate choice. Grad school was expensive. New York was expensive. I only had the opportunity to work on campus at the time. I did everything possible though. I worked for a few months as a volunteer research assistant to establish some credentials in New York at the graduate school. I worked away as a library assistant, shelving books in Butler during winter break and onwards to earn money. I maxed out the amount of time allotted to me, did an excellent job so I would be able to keep on working (and indeed I was given more hours than all other people), so I could even pay the rent and living expenses there. I also worked as an administrative assistant while writing my thesis, jamming for classes, and participating in all the social activities to bond and see what people at I-House where I was living were doing, worked hard to earn scholarships and such because they are indeed a source of income for you, and you earn them through your own work and talents. That is the difficult and rewarding part. It is like running your life as your own business. People are often cash-strapped, but that is important because you can either feel defeated and do not do anything consequently, or you can garner so much more motivation to win and work harder every day.

I chose the latter. And I think it worked out, so at least I could manage to have my Master's degree, learned what I wanted to learn, saw what I wanted to see, and had my surgery while in graduate school so I could move on to other new projects. At 23-24 at the time and figured all that out all by myself, I think it was a decent accomplishment. I overcame the biggest challenge, the unknown for me, which was the gender reassignment surgery, and it worked out pretty fine after that. Still lots of challenges to go, but that was the biggest thing and I got it done. It was a relief and a great thing to feel, because it can haunt you for the rest of your life if you do not get it done.

So you too. If you need to work and study in order to get your Bachelor's, your Master's, your PhDs, JDs, or MDs, or anything else, do not hesitate. If you really want to have it, you will have it. Through hard work and determination, anything can be possible for you. And education is always so important, so necessary, and go far beyond the professional skills, the practicality that you may need on a day-to-day basis. We need people who can think. We need people, not robots anyways, so get an education and you will be much grateful for it later on. Nothing comes out of a vacuum, but if you want something and really work hard for it, in a legal and honest way, then you can achieve your own goal. And it feels great.

When I started the law school in France, I loved law so much but I also wanted to start exploring the professional world, and earn money to support myself obviously. It was tough. I had to take a year off my second year to concentrate on working to pay the bills and build work experience. The third year, I came back to school, worked during the day and went to classes in the evening. I read, studied. France had its different way of teaching and learning, and the language issue, writing like a law student at the best law school in France, was not easy. But validating the diploma was symbolic, and very important for me also. Eventually, I took an entire week to study and obviously passed all the Common Law exams as well as an oral exam on comparative penal law in French, which covered pretty much all sorts of penal laws in different countries. Still much to go, but it was a fantastic feeling and at the end of the day. So critical to accomplish these goals in life, because they mean something to you and you just have to get it done properly through more work. Plan carefully and push your best efforts, because you never know what will happen at the end. But one thing for sure, it will definitely be something better than not doing anything at all.

Of course there will be people out there who will be bad-mouthing about me or my book. But I hope they too can learn from this book and become a better person.

At least I dare to be myself to show that I am a young, talented and independent woman. I work hard to bring out the best in me, and I dare to keep on improving myself. That is much better than being lazy, dependent, and creating problems rather than create positive force for other people who need encouragement in their lives.

I am grateful thinking about my parents. After the Vietnam War, they started from zero in South Vietnam with nothing, before building everything from their hands by becoming entrepreneurs and entered the textile industry at the time. They made courageous decisions to be entrepreneurs. I might not agree with them on many issues, but I admired my Dad for his vision, and my Mom for the tireless hard work she gave to my Dad and our family.

There are things in life that only you can do, and situations only you can help yourself. Take advantage of the self-help opportunities out there to build something independently. Everything is possible within your imagination and your efforts to make it come true. A dream is a wish your heart makes after all.

Forever and Always A Girl
by Hung Huynh
May 2022

CPSIA information can be obtained
at www.ICGtesting.com
Printed in the USA
BVHW051848090822
644140BV00006B/337